EEQ
Exceptional Education Quarterly

Observations and Meanings of Difference: Measurement of Exceptionality

ASPEN SYSTEMS CORPORATION

EEQ Exceptional Education Quarterly

An Aspen Publication®

Publisher: Theodore Caris
Editor-in-Chief: John R. Marozsan
Editorial Director: R. Curtis Whitesel
Managing Editor: Margot S. Raphael
Associate Editor: Connie Braundmeier

Editorial Assistant: Ellen Gerecht
Production Manager: Paul R. Carlin
Advertising Manager: Joseph Del Master
Manager Fulfillment Operations:
Ernest V. Manzella, Jr.

EXCEPTIONAL EDUCATION QUARTERLY (ISSN 0196-6960) is published quarterly by Aspen Systems Corporation, 1600 Research Boulevard, Rockville, MD 20850. Second-class postage is paid at Germantown, Maryland, and additional mailing offices. POSTMASTER: Send address changes to Aspen Systems Corporation, P.O. Box 486, Gaithersburg, MD 20760.

Subscription Rates: $30.00 per year in the United States and Canada (four issues). Payable in advance. Subscribers may specify a particular issue to begin the subscription if desired. **Subscribers in United Kingdom, Europe, Middle East and Africa:** Aspen Systems Corporation, 3 Henrietta Street, London WC2E 8LU, ENGLAND. Delivered subscription prices available upon request. **Subscribers in Japan:** Address subscription inquiries to Maruzen Company, Ltd., P.O. Box 5050, Tokyo International, 100-31, JAPAN.

Editorial correspondence, letters to the editor and manuscript submissions should be addressed to: Editorial Director, EEQ, Aspen Systems Corporation, 1600 Research Boulevard, Rockville, MD 20850.

Business correspondence (subscription inquiries, subscription orders, change of address, etc.) should be addressed to Fulfillment Operations, Aspen Systems Corporation, P.O. Box 486, Gaithersburg, MD 20760.

Notices for change of address, including the subscriber's old and new address, should be sent to Fulfillment Operations, Aspen Systems Corporation, P.O. Box 486, Gaithersburg, MD 20760 six weeks in advance of effective date.

Student, Intern, Resident Subscription: $20.00 a year payable in advance. A qualifying letter from school or institution is required and must accompany the order.

Single Copies: $13.50 each; enclose payment with order. **Multiple Copies for Educational and Training Programs:** Inquiries from bona fide educational programs concerning terms of sale will be answered promptly. Send inquiries to: Fulfillment Operations, Aspen Systems Corporation, P.O. Box 486, Gaithersburg, MD 20760.

Advertising: Direct all inquiries and correspondence to Advertising Manager, P.O. Box 643, Spring Lake, NJ 07762, Telephone: (201) 775-4522.

Issue: Vol. 1, No. 3 ISBN: 0-89443-402-0
ISSN: 0196-6960
Printed in the United States of America.

Contents

Editorial Board

Letters to the Editor

All letters to the editor should be addressed to Editor, EEQ, Aspen Systems Corporation, 1600 Research Boulevard, Rockville, MD 20850. Unless otherwise stated, we assume that letters addressed to the editor are intended for publication with your name and affiliation. As many letters as possible will be published. When space is limited and we cannot publish all letters received, we will select letters reflecting the range of opinions and ideas received. If a letter merits a response from an author or the editor, we will obtain a reply and publish both letters.

From the Editor

Special education became a public enterprise because education officials and teachers observed marked differences among children. The observed variability among children was recognized as the central problem of special education in the first general special education text published in this country (Horn, 1924). I think it is accurate to say that the observation of differences among children and the meanings we attach to those differences are matters we have never been able to deal with adequately as professionals or as members of American society.

As professionals, we have demonstrated little finesse in measurement of those differences that are educationally relevant. During the past two decades we have begun to give up our unthinking acceptance of claims for reliability, validity, and instructional value of psychological and educational tests and other measurement devices. But today many professionals are mesmerized by the inane propositions that all tests are worthless and that any means of educational evaluation resulting in the disproportionate representation of any minority group, including the handicapped, is inherently invalid and prejudicial.

As members of American society, we have sensed a renewed commitment during the past two decades to the ideals of equal protection of law and equal opportunity. But measurement always points out differences—inequalities—and we are tempted merely to deny the validity of measured differences that do not correspond to our egalitarian ideals or to how we wish the world to be.

To the extent that education is a science, the problem of measurement is a pervasive concern of teachers. An applied science cannot be developed beyond its techniques for measuring the phenomena with which it deals. Thus progress in measurement—in observing difference in teaching and learning—is essential for advancing the science of education. We can become better at educating exceptional children only as we become better at measuring what teachers do, what children learn, and how measures of teaching and learning are related.

To the extent that education is an instrument of social policy, measurement of educational characteristics and outcomes must serve the objectives of the state. Perhaps nowhere is this made clearer than in PL 94-142. Social policy as embodied in this law, the rules and regulations accompanying it, and related law and litigation increasingly determine when, by whom, for what purpose, by what means, and with what outcome children's educational differences will be observed. The prescriptions and proscriptions of measurement dictated by social policy are written to assure that our ideals of equal protection and equal opportunity are upheld. As a free and equitable society, we cannot condone educational measurement that is irrelevant, biased, or denigrating of the individual.

This issue of EEQ deals with both professional and social policy problems. The content of the issue illustrates the fact that social policy questions have become paramount. It is tempting to hope that we are entering a new era in special education, one in which the decisions and guidelines of centralized government will ensure that children's differences are observed rightly. Whether that hope is well founded will depend on our personal and professional character and on the character of our society. As Hungerford (1950) said in his essay on human sameness and difference, "only the brave dare look upon difference without flinching" (p. 417).

REFERENCES

Horn, J.L. *The education of exceptional children.* New York: Century, 1924.

Hungerford, R.H. On locusts. *American Journal of Mental Deficiency,* 1950, *54,* 415-418.

James Kauffman
Editor

Foreword

No other single topic in special education has commanded as much attention and controversy as measurement strategies used with handicapped students. While the measurement of exceptionality has always been a difficult undertaking, current social, political, professional, and legal factors have combined to make the evaluation of the handicapped an extremely arduous task.

Almost every special educator is aware of the many court cases questioning the legality of some measurement techniques and devices used in deciding students' needs for special education services. Recent federal and state laws and regulations have drastically altered the orientation of many traditional measurement policies used in the nation's schools. Measurement techniques based on different theoretical viewpoints are continually being produced. The accurate and precise measurement of exceptionality remains the most difficult professional task demanded of special educators.

Measurement is best defined as a process involving the assignment of values (i.e., numbers) to attributes or characteristics of persons or events according to explicit guidelines or rules. In education, the precise observations required by measurement will usually be achieved through (a) standardized tests, (b) criterion-referenced surveys, and (c) structured observations carried out in controlled settings under prearranged conditions.

The data generated from these measurement strategies are used in several ways in special education. The first and most obvious reason for collecting measurement information is to identify handicapped students and place them in the most appropriate educational setting.

Once identification and placement are accomplished, measurement data are used to determine students' strengths and weaknesses to establish the goals and content of remedial programming. The students' progress in the selected program will be continually monitored by measuring performance, and curriculum modifications will be undertaken if necessary. Research and theory development is a final use of measurement information. Measurement activities are clearly the backbone of many facets of special education and consequently are important to any professional concerned with handicapped individuals.

This issue of EEQ addresses several major issues currently affecting the measurement of exceptionality in the schools. These issues include (a) legal and administrative problems; (b) competence of persons conducting the measurement activities; (c) nondiscriminatory testing; (d) measurement of cognitive abilities; and (e) models and practices dealing specifically with the measurement of functional competencies of the adolescent, measurement within the curriculum, and assessment of the severely and profoundly handicapped.

The first two articles provide an overview and discussion of the administrative and legal aspects of measurement and evaluation in the school. Bradley and Howe address the effects of litigation, negotiation, and legislation on the administration of special education programming at the state level. Martin, an attorney, provides a broader perspective on the effect of major federal legislation on handicapped children and their parents. McNutt and Mandelbaum comprehensively analyze the skills necessary to perform educational assessments. The authors devote particular attention to the philosophies and abilities of the tester. General measurement competencies are grouped according to technique, application, and synthesis.

Oakland examines the problems inherent in the assessment of minority group children. He delineates possible bias points that can affect measurement decisions before, during, and after the evaluation has been conducted. Reid and Hresko then carefully point out the fallacy in using quantitative measurements to judge students' learning and teachers' knowledge. The limitations of standardized tests to direct teaching are specifically discussed.

The last three articles focus on the measurement of functional competencies and the handicapped; informal assessment of student progress in special education curriculum; and evaluation of the severely and profoundly handicapped. Wiederholt, Cronin, and Stubbs discuss the construct of functional competency from the standpoint of current assessment practices. They conclude that the concept of competency is currently not well understood and that measurement practices in this area vary widely. Poplin and Gray provide an innovative approach to the classification of educational curriculum and the informal assessment of student progress within the curriculum. Dollar and Brooks present an in-depth discussion of the identification, program evaluation, and educational measurement of the severely and profoundly handicapped.

I believe that the information presented in this issue of EEQ is not available in any other single source. I hope each article will stimulate theoreticians and practitioners to produce more philosophically sound instruments and techniques that are technically rigorous and useful in planning and evaluating remedial strategies for the handicapped. Accountability in measurement will continue to be of great concern for educators. Professionals must therefore increase their knowledge of research on measurement. If the information available from new research is not broadly used, the measurement of exceptionality will remain a frequently haphazard process.

Stephen Larsen
Issue Editor

Administrative Issues in Evaluation of Exceptionality

Carol McDanolds Bradley
Iowa State Department of Public
   Instruction
Des Moines, Iowa

Clifford E. Howe
University of Iowa
Iowa City, Iowa

BEFORE THE MID-1960s, a special education administrator was expected to know theory and practice in special education and administration. Since then litigation, legislation, and negotiation have become additional areas of knowledge essential for one's survival in special education administration. Such knowledge is particularly critical in the evaluation of exceptionality.

EFFECTS OF LITIGATION

Bersoff (1979) has convincingly detailed the use of testing in racial and ethnic discrimination in the schools following the *Brown v. Board of Education* decision, (347 U.S. 483 [1954]). He points out that for most people scores derived from psychometric instruments have historically been used for exclusionary purposes. In *Hobsen v. Hansen* (269 F. Supp. 401 [D.D.C. 1967]) the court ordered abolishment of a tracking system based

0196-6960/80/0013-0001$2.00
© 1980 Aspen Systems Corporation

1

primarily on tests that were standardized for predominantly white, middle-class students. The court had found vastly disproportionate numbers of black children in the lower tracks and no evidence that they were receiving any compensatory education so that they might gain access to higher tracks.

Administrator's Quandary

Diana v. California Department of Education (C.A. No. C-70 37 RFP) involved the identification of Mexican-American students as educable mentally retarded (EMR) and their subsequent placement in EMR classes. The plaintiffs contested the use of the Wechsler Intelligence Scale for Children (WISC) and Stanford-Binet tests in determining their ability to learn. The two parties entered into a consent decree. It stipulated that assessment prior to placement in EMR classes would involve an intelligence test, developmental history, educational evaluation, and adaptive behavior scale. This decree, the work of Mercer and others, and the position of the American Association on Mental Deficiency have resulted in most state definitions of mental retardation including a deficit in adaptive behavior component. Assessment of adaptive behavior is required, but so much controversy surrounds the issue that the administrator is in a quandary about which direction to take: (a) What instruments should be used? (b) Are different instruments required for varied ethnic and social groups? (c) Do the best known current instruments discriminate against rural and suburban middle-class

students? (d) What type of diagnostic personnel are best trained to administer tests and interpret such assessment data?

Slighting Adaptive Behavior

On the issue of adaptive behavior it is instructive to look at the work of Smith and Polloway (1979). They examined the subject selection procedures and subject descriptions in all research using mentally retarded persons published in the *American Journal of Mental Deficiency* from 1974 through 1978. They found that only 5.8% of the 374 research reports included measures of both intellectual functioning and adaptive behavior in subject descriptors. In an additional 3.7% of the studies, researchers reported some measure of adaptive behavior but did not always specify the instrument used. Smith and Polloway reported no marked increase over the five-year period in the number of research reports including both measures; each year a single measure of intelligence or mental age was the most common form of subject selection and description.

The major explanation for this finding is probably the increased time required for obtaining measures of adaptive behavior directly and the use by researchers of readily available data already collected by the schools. It seems to us, though, that researchers should lead the way for the practicing administrator in this endeavor.

Scrutinizing Standardized Tests

More recently, in *Larry P. v. Riles* (343 F. Supp. 1306 [N.D. Cal. 1972] aff'd 502

F. 2d 963 [9th Cir. 1974]) the court ordered that the California Department of Education's chief administrator was "enjoined from utilizing, permitting the use of, or approving the use of any standardized intelligence tests for the identification of black EMR children or their placement into EMR classes, without securing prior approval by the court" (p. 104).

To obtain court approval, a written request must be submitted that details, among other items, that the tests are not racially or culturally discriminatory, will be administered in a manner that is nondiscriminatory in its effect on black children, and have been validated for the determination of EMR status or placement in EMR classes. The court also ordered the defendants to direct each school district to reevaluate every black child currently identified as an EMR pupil without using any standardized intelligence test that had not been approved by the court.

The court expressed reluctance to get involved but wrote in the introduction: "The history of this litigation has demonstrated the failure of legislators and administrative agencies to confront problems that clearly had to be faced, and it has revealed an all-too-typical willingness either to do nothing or to pass on issues to the court" (p. 2).

At this point the directions for administrators seem fairly obvious:

- Do not use standardized academic or intelligence tests if they may result in the placement of minority children in EMR classes or special "tracks" disproportionate to their number in the general school population.

"The history of this litigation has revealed an all-too-typical willingness either to do nothing or to pass on issues to the Court." (quote from legal decision)

- Use nonbiased assessment procedures that are culturally fair and valid for the purpose intended.
- Use multiple measures, including developmental history, educational evaluations, and adaptive behavior scales.
- Understand that assessment instruments and procedures are under the scrutiny of the court.

Before an administrator becomes too comfortable with these "directions," two other cases need to be reviewed.

A Goal for the 1980s

In 1976 in *Frederick L. v. Thomas* (408 F. Supp. 832 [E. D. Pa. 1976]) the court interpreted "right to education" to include screening and evaluation for potentially learning disabled children. Part of the evidence in this case involved expert witness testimony for both sides that 3% was probably the prevalence of learning disabilities in the Philadelphia schools. This prevalence estimate would indicate approximately 7,900 learning disabled children, but only 1,300 were receiving special services.

The December 24, 1979, issue of *Education Daily* reported that a U.S. district court had ordered the New York City schools to evaluate and place 8,000 children *within 60 days*. The order applied to 2,000 children who had been referred for evaluation and another 6,000 handicapped students awaiting placement in special education programs.

Administrators face a series of questions, if not dilemmas, in reconciling the "directions" with these two cases, including:

1. How is it possible to evaluate 2,000 children appropriately in 60 days and meet the culture-fair, nondiscriminatory, valid, multiple-measure criteria?

2. How does one screen for potential learning disabilities without using standardized tests when teacher referral as a source has been exhausted?

3. How does one evaluate for suspected learning disabilities without using standardized intelligence tests when an essential criterion in determining learning disability is a significant discrepancy between ability and achievement (remember the 60 days)?

4. Is it permissible to use data from standardized academic and intelligence tests to support a finding of "nonhandicapped"?

It is easy to understand why some special education administrators believe the solution is to eliminate the need for classification by handicapping condition, describe children in terms of their unique needs, and presumably develop multiple alternatives to deliver appropriate education to all.

While these are worthy goals, special education administrators need to be certain their motivation is in behalf of children and not an embarrassed reaction to scrutiny of practices in special education that have been less than professional, a fear of being sued, or a wish to shift the total responsibility to the general education administrator now that accountability is a watchword. Eliminating the necessity of determining that students are handicapped in obtaining an education could also eliminate children's hard-won rights to education under the law. A more reasonable approach is to work diligently to see that rights afforded the handicapped minority are extended to the majority of students in America's schools. If all students and their parents had the right by law to be involved in decisions regarding evaluation and selection of appropriate educational alternatives, the need for "special" or "protected" classifications would be eliminated.

It remains to be seen whether society at large will make this type of investment in the education of its youth. Such an investment seems doubtful in a time of high inflation, taxpayer revolt, and energy and defense crises. It is a worthy goal for the 1980s—one special education administrators should diligently pursue.

EFFECTS OF LEGISLATION

The protection of PL 94-142 accrues only to students "suspected" of being

If all students and their parents had the right by law to be involved in decisions regarding evaluation and selection of appropriate educational alternatives, the need for "special" or "protected" classifications would be eliminated.

handicapped and those who have been determined to be handicapped and in need of special education and related services. This statute and accompanying regulations require that pupils be identified by the familiar categories. The regulations go on to define these categories. Clearly, such classification and eligibility criteria were spelled out for the purpose of narrowing the potential number of clients and thus controlling associated costs.

Similar criteria exist at the state level. Because local school district budgets have been so strapped recently, many states have accepted the responsibility of developing legislation that provides most of the excess costs of educating handicapped students. Legislators ask and expect answers to questions about who these handicapped children are, how many there are, and what their appropriate education will cost. They expect some consistency and uniformity across a state, usually calling for definitions and procedures to be well detailed.

Grasping the Need for Improvement

It seems, then, that an immediate effect of this legislation is an understanding that practices in evaluation of exceptionality or potential exceptionality must be greatly improved. In the near future, practicing administrators, who daily face questions about measurement of exceptionality— questions that have no answers—should be the greatest supporters of research and evaluation in this area.

New Safeguards, New Questions

Because of reported abuses in the evaluation process, Congress wrote into PL 94-142 a number of procedural safeguards regarding testing and evaluation. Most notably, each child suspected of being handicapped is to receive a full and individual evaluation. This was augmented by regulations adopted by the Office for Special Education and Rehabilitative Services (formerly Bureau of Education for the Handicapped), which delineated specific evaluation procedures that must be met. Included were requirements that test and evaluation materials (a) be provided and administered in the child's native language or other mode of communication, if feasible; (b) be valid for the purpose for which they are used; (c) be given in a standardized way by properly trained personnel; (d) include those tailored to assess specific areas of educational need rather than just those providing a single, general intelligence quotient; (e) be ones that accurately reflect the factors that the tests claim they measure. Regulations specify that the evaluation is to be made by a multidisciplinary team and not by a single examiner. Also, handicapped students are to be reevaluated at least every three years according to the same requirements.

These regulations immediately raised and continue to provoke tough questions for the practicing administrator:

- How do I locate diagnosticians who speak languages other than English when I need them?
- Is an interpreter for those doing the

6

assessment sufficient to meet the requirements of the law?

- What instruments and procedures are "valid enough?"
- How can I ensure that assessments are done in a standardized way? No short forms? No extrapolation?
- Who are the "properly trained" personnel? Every specialty area believes that *its* professionals are best trained.
- What constitutes a multidisciplinary team? How many disciplines? Each discipline believes that it is essential.
- If the child is still "obviously" handicapped, must the reevaluation be so comprehensive, especially in light of data already available in the annual review of the individualized education program?

Jones (1978) argues that these regulations apply to group testing programs as well as to individual evaluations. This assertion rests on the premise that group testing programs and individual testing procedures are interrelated in the sense that results from group testing are sometimes the first level of identification of children who may need specialized services. Also, any composite educational picture of an individual pupil includes group test results.

Inappropriate Labeling of Minorities

These rather restrictive regulations stemmed from a history of inappropriate labeling of some children as handicapped, principally Mexican and black students. Ysseldyke (1978) recently reviewed this issue of bias in assessment and concluded that the concerns were much broader than just fairness of tests used with minority groups. Various abuses or misuses of assessment data throughout the whole process of making decisions about pupils are of concern. He summarized these abuses as including (a) use of tests for purposes other than those for which they were designed, (b) comparison of students with others who differ systematically in several characteristics, (c) use of technically inadequate tests, and (d) making inferences that go beyond the data (p. 159).

Administrators and teachers are frustrated by their additional responsibilities. At the same time, appropriations have fallen far short of the accelerating funding schedule authorized by Congress in the original bill. There is some suggestion that school officials are not actively identifying additional children who may be handicapped and in need of special education because of the attendant time and dollar costs as well as the prospect of parental disagreement and due-process proceedings (see Magliocca & Stephens, 1980). The time-honored practice of putting children on waiting lists creates all types of legal problems today.

To retain sanity and stay in the business, administrators must strike a reasonable balance between the fear of being sued and of protecting the rights of handicapped pupils in relation to evaluation and identification under the provisions of PL 94-142 (see also Bateman & Herr, in press; Ysseldyke & Shinn, in press).

Satisfying "Irrelevant Demands"

As funds become more scarce, the amount of personnel time (thus money) spent on identification practices aimed at determining eligibility for additional public funding becomes more questionable. Larsen (1977) points out, "evaluation is all too often undertaken to satisfy generally irrelevant administrative demands that are extraneous to the main purpose of teaching" (p. 123).

While there may be differences of opinion about the relevance of procedural safeguards and adequate financing, we would certainly not argue that much current practice in evaluation is not focused on the teaching and learning process. Assessment procedures must be developed, used, and evaluated that can, whenever possible, serve the dual purpose of identification and instructional program planning. Data from these procedures need to be of use whether or not the pupil is found to be handicapped. Without doubt, much of the assessment data must come from extensive observations of students in natural settings and less from formal tests given in isolated settings. This will require diagnosticians to have broad mastery of the education field; they will not be able to rely on skills acquired only in narrow specialty-area training programs. The need for assessment data to serve the purposes of identification and instructional program planning and the competition for scarce fiscal resources will provide momentum for the well-trained special educator to serve also as a primary diagnostician (see articles by Meyen & Lehr, EEQ 1:2, and Poplin & Gray, this issue).

Problems for Administrators

Administrators face problems relating to staffing patterns, new personnel selec-

tion, and the need for retraining existing diagnostic personnel. There will not be a role in the future for school psychologists, who give only WISC and Stanford-Binet tests, speech clinicians, who rely on Wepmans and the Illinois Test of Psycholinguistic Abilities, or educational diagnosticians who depend on Wide-Range Achievement Test and Peabody Individual Achievement Test to assess present levels of educational functioning.

PERSONNEL DECISIONS

Administrators must make decisions about what type of personnel are necessary to the evaluation process and how many of each type are needed. These decisions must be made in partial ignorance; administrators are not and cannot be experts in all aspects of evaluation. Various educational professions cannot be relied on to help with this decision. The members of each discipline seem to believe the solution lies in employing more people just like them! Furthermore, one cannot discount the self-serving interests of groups to protect their own employment status.

Once administrators decide how many and what types of diagnostic personnel to employ, they must decide how to deploy them. To whom a referral is first made can significantly contribute to the eventual disposition of the case. Some administrators have set up referral processing teams to guard against the "gatekeeper" phenomenon by one discipline as well as to preclude unnecessary and routinized evaluation by a host of varying specialists in all cases.

8   ACHIEVING UNIFORMITY IN EVALUATIONS

Another perplexity involves achieving a reasonable degree of uniformity or consistency in evaluation practices across districts or even buildings within a single district. Those who have spent considerable time in the public schools know that a pupil who is viewed as a candidate for referral for evaluation of a suspected disability in one building or district might well not be viewed in that way by the staff of another school. There seems also to be a tendency for the faculty of an individual building or small district to view pupils' suspected disabilities in terms of the types of programs they have available for children. This is seen in referrals that state "evaluation needed for learning disabilities program" or "evaluate for resource room program." Students are too often labeled to conform to local building programs rather than evaluated for problems that could involve transportation to a more appropriate program 20 miles away.

ALTERNATIVES TO RELOCATION

These "at home" solutions are appropriate in some individual circumstances. Some schools have developed alternatives within general education in which mildly handicapped pupils particularly are appropriately included. Some teachers can and do adjust their expectations, curriculum, and instructional strategies to accommodate a wide range of individual differences. Other faculty understand their students so well that they can accurately predict suspected disabilities and know which program options would be appropriate. Special education adminis-trators need to reinforce and encourage such practices.

However, it would be a mistake to assume that low referral rates necessarily indicate positive attitudes and appropriate education for the potentially handicapped of a given building or district. There are too many instances of social promotion and even graduation without students' having acquired essential survival skills to believe that all children are being properly educated (see article by Pullin, EEQ 1:2). Dropout rates in many areas are increasing. Youth unemployment rates, particularly for the black and poor, have reached alarming proportions. Absenteeism, tardiness, and truancy are often highest in schools with generally lower-than-average achievement levels, possibly the very same schools with lower referral rates.

MORE QUESTIONS

A number of questions about locating the potentially handicapped under such conditions must be addressed:

- Should more reliance be placed on screening programs and less on teacher referral?
- If so, what screening procedures can be developed that are time and cost efficient and do not yield large numbers of false positives?
- Would a "child find" media campaign aimed at student self-referral be more productive and less costly?
- Should a far more active campaign be launched to reach parents who are not easy to reach, such as those who do not belong to PTA, advocacy groups, Lions, or Rotary?

- Is more in-service training the answer?
- Is a building-based special education teacher the best person to screen potentially handicapped individuals?

The reverse of low referrals occurs when districts, schools, or teachers view all students not at grade level as potentially handicapped and therefore refer many of their students for evaluation. This problem should lessen as the least-restrictive-environment concept becomes fully implemented. There is increasingly less chance that such referrals will result in total removal of mildly handicapped pupils from the classroom, building, or district. This should remove the motivation to make such wholesale referrals on the hope that the "problem child" will leave or at least be someone else's responsibility. Admittedly, there is no magical cutoff point separating the handicapped from the so-called normal child. The greatest conflicts appear with youngsters in the borderline areas.

ENVIRONMENTAL FACTORS

A major shortcoming of educational evaluation has been "the tendency to ignore the significant variables of the student's immediate environment in causing and maintaining academic and/or social problems" (Larsen, 1977, p. 130). In addition to the benefits of an ecological assessment model as enumerated by Larsen, this type of assessment is absolutely essential in helping to determine who is *not* handicapped. Assessment data taken across environments, persons, curricular areas, and instructional conditions can identify system defects or personnel problems that need remediation instead of a child who needs special education. Again, the primary purpose of evaluation should be to aid in instructional programing, not to "sort" who qualifies for additional monies.

EFFECTS OF NEGOTIATION

Negotiation is broadly defined here to mean conferring, discussing, or bargaining to reach agreements. It includes concepts such as group process, shared decision making, and participative management, as well as the formal collective bargaining process.

Many, if not most, currently practicing administrators were trained to function in bureaucratic organizations under a hierarchical authority model (Herda, 1980). Within school systems, special education administrators often operated independently of general education administrators; in effect, dual systems were in place. Further, there tended to be a distinct separation between special education and other public and private agencies serving the handicapped. Special education administrators typically were not trained for nor had much experience in sharing responsibility or authority with staff or peers. They were not prepared to negotiate—to confer, discuss, or bargain to reach agreements. Administrators did not understand that one positive way to influence others is to share power. Events of the last 10 years have demanded that special education administrators quickly come to terms with these requirements for competent performance.

10

The Team Approach

PL 94-142 requires a multidisciplinary evaluation team; presumably a "team" will confer, discuss, and reach agreements that are better than a single individual's judgment. This outcome (better decisions) is not guaranteed just because a group of people are involved. A team implies something more than—and successful functioning as a team member requires an additional set of skills beyond—technical adequacy in evaluation processes.

Administrators' new responsibility is to recruit and employ diagnostic personnel who have the additional group process and communication skills necessary to function effectively as a team. Provisions will have to be made for in-service or continuing education programs for currently employed personnel. Administrators need to develop and implement personnel evaluation systems that attend to these factors for use in contract renewal, salary, promotion, and termination decisions.

New Skills and Attitudes

The administrator is not exempt from needing to quickly acquire these new

---

The administrator's new responsibility is to recruit and employ diagnostic personnel who have the additional group process and communication skills necessary to function effectively as a team.

---

skills and attitudes. Implementation of effective and cost-efficient referral and evaluation mechanisms is a system wide responsibility. To accomplish this, the special education administrator must give up independent decision making and work with general education administrators on a co-equal basis.

The special education administrator must learn that working with disgruntled parents and their advocates does not have to be adversarial. Generally, there is more than one solution to every problem; by conferring, discussing, and even bargaining, a compromise position can be reached that is appropriate for the child and satisfactory to the school and the parents.

As access to special education has broadened to include children from age 3 (birth, in some states) to 21, the special education administrator will be working increasingly with other agencies that serve the handicapped. Inevitably problems of "turfmanship" will surface. The only way to solve these problems is by joint decision making, probably prefaced by long hours of discourse. Particular examples of issues administrators will face relative to evaluation include

- Accepting another agency's determination of disability;
- Avoiding duplication of screening efforts, particularly with infants and young children;
- Varying criteria for determination of disability—for example, mental health authorities, vocational rehabilitation;
- Assessing potentially handicapped youth in correctional facilities.

Results of Collective Bargaining

Most states now have laws permitting or requiring collective bargaining for public employees. Attitudes of special education administrators toward collective bargaining seem to run the gamut from the "chicken little" pessimistic outlook to those who see this new era as an opportunity to develop a more humane and fair system of participatory decision making. Following are examples of items that have been included in collective bargaining negotiations that can affect the evaluation of exceptionality:

- The setting of class size limitations that double count handicapped students integrated into regular classrooms. This could affect teachers' willingness to refer and their subsequent identification of pupils as handicapped.
- Determining what is to be included in in-service training programs and setting limits in terms of time, frequency, and length of faculty meetings. How does one find adequate time to provide in-service programs on evaluation procedures?
- Limiting parent conferences in terms of frequency, purpose, and time. What happens when the parents can meet only after 5 p.m. and the contract day ends at 4:15 p.m.?
- Mandating referrals of students to other personnel. To the degree that the item negotiated involves the degree and amount of aberrant behavior to be tolerated in a regular classroom, operational definitions of "handicap" and "requiring special education" could be affected.
- Determining the ratio of supportive personnel to teaching staff or dictating their modes of operation within the school. Each of these areas traditionally has been an administrative prerogative.

Of course, items cannot be negotiated that are contrary to state and federal law. Nevertheless, the special education administrator must quickly acquire understandings and skills in the negotiation process so as not to be bewildered and ineffectual through the 1980s.

SUMMARY

This article has attempted to examine the effects of three relatively new phenomena in education—litigation, legislation, and negotiation—on the evaluation of exceptionality from an administrative view. We have raised more questions than we have answered. The questions must be answered in the decade ahead. This decade will not be a comfortable one for many administrators. It will not be for the faint hearted. It will be an exciting one.

12 REFERENCES

Bateman, B., & Herr, C. Law and special education. In J. M. Kauffman & D. P. Hallahan (Eds.), *Handbook of special education*. Englewood Cliffs, N.J.: Prentice-Hall, in press.

Bersoff, N. Regarding psychologists testily: Legal regulations of psychological assessment in the public schools. In B. Sales & M. Novick (Eds.), *Perspectives in law and psychology*, Vol. III: *Testing and evaluation*. New York: Plenum, 1979.

Education Daily, 12(245) Washington, D.C.: Capitol Publications, 1979.

Herda, E. A. Aspects of general education governance and PL 94-142 implementation. *Focus on Exceptional Children*, 1980, 12(5).

Jones, R. J. Protection in evaluation procedures: criteria and recommendations. In *Developing criteria for the evaluation of protection in evaluation procedures provisions*. Washington, D.C.: United States Office of Education, 1978.

Larsen, S. C. The educational evaluation of handicapped students. In R. Kneedler & S. Tarver (Eds.), *Changing perspectives in special education*. Columbus, Ohio: Charles E. Merrill, 1977.

Magliocca, L. A., & Stephens, T. M. Child identification or child inventory? A critique of the federal design of child-identification systems implemented under PL 94-142. *Journal of Special Education*, 1980, *14*, 23-36.

Smith, J. D., & Polloway, E. The dimension of adaptive behavior in mental retardation research: An analysis of recent practices. *American Journal of Mental Deficiency*, 1979, *84*, 203-206.

Ysseldyke, J. E. Implementing the "protection in evaluation procedures" provisions of Public Law 94-142. In *Developing criteria for the evaluation of protection in evaluation procedures provisions*. Washington, D.C.: United States Office of Education, 1978.

Ysseldyke, J., & Shinn, M. Psychoeducational diagnosis. In J.M. Kauffman & D. P. Hallahan (Eds.), *Handbook of special education*. Englewood Cliffs, N.J.: Prentice-Hall, in press.

Legal Issues in Assessment for Special Education

Reed Martin
Attorney
Houston, Texas

FEDERAL LEGISLATION and judicial decisions have changed the roles of special education evaluators. The traditional diagnostic role has been broadened. Professionals may find themselves in a new role as "independent evaluators." Prescription decision making is shared among many in the new forum called the individualized education program (IEP) planning meeting. In addition, evaluators will likely be required to participate in emergency disciplinary proceedings and called to testify in the administrative trials known as impartial hearings.

THE GOOD OLD DAYS

Not many years ago schools asked evaluators to perform in an individual effort. An evaluator using a single criterion often made judgments that brought about dramatic changes in children's lives. Testing instruments were often normed on

0196-6960/80/0013-0013$2.00
© 1980 Aspen Systems Corporation

13

14

children so unlike the subjects being assessed that serious cultural and racial bias issues were raised. The administrators of tests received virtually no instruction in accommodating the needs of the handicapped; and, as a consequence, it was not unusual to find bright learning disabled or physically impaired children who were erroneously thought to have intelligence in the retarded range.

The diagnostic label hung on a child dictated the placement in which services were offered and thus carried the potential to be a self-fulfilling prophecy. Reevaluation typically occurred on a triannual cycle, so mistakes could be felt for a long time. Such mistakes were shielded from the check and balance of nonprofessional scrutiny because schools jealously guarded their files, stamping them "for professional use only." They routinely turned down parents' requests to find out what was being written about their child.

Communication with parents was typically minimal. For example, the author met a woman who had been told simply that her son was in an EMR program. She deduced that EMR stood for English, math, and reading—which were indeed the three areas in which her child was weakest! Professionals often laugh appreciatively at that true story, thinking it says something about the intelligence of the parent. Rather, it says something about the school.

COURT CASES AND LEGISLATION

A dramatic change in the not-so-good old days began in California in the early 1970s. Revelations that large numbers of black children were being swept into classes for the retarded on the basis of a single administration of an intelligence test led to the filing of a law suit, *Larry P. v. Riles* (343 F. Supp. 1306 [N.D. Cal. 1972] aff'd 502 F.2d 963 [9th Cir. 1974]). The preliminary relief granted in *Larry P.* banned placements on the basis of a single criterion. Although the case did not reach a final decision for another 7 years (3 EHLR 551:295, N.D. Cal. 1979), it had alerted the country and Congress to a serious problem.

Revelations about parents' being denied permission to see their children's records also came to the attention of Congress. The resulting Buckley Amendment became the Family Education Rights and Privacy Act (PL 93-380, codified at 20 U.S.C. 1232g, with implementing regulations at 45 C.F.R. 99). The resulting right of access gave parents an opportunity to see all information that affects evaluation, placement, or programming of their children. The right extends to all personally identifiable educational records collected, maintained, and used by the school, without regard to who within the school system has possession of the file. Further, parents can demand a change in any record they find inaccurate, misleading, or violating their privacy.

During the first half of the 1970s Congress passed two other significant pieces of legislation influencing evaluation: the Education for All Handicapped Children Act of 1975 (PL 94-142) and Section 504 of the Rehabilitation Act of 1973. Legislative history makes clear the congressional concern over nonbiased diagnoses and effective prescriptions.

THE EVALUATION PROCESS

All schools have standard referral processes that are used when a teacher's observation or other screening technique identifies a child as in need of evaluation. But PL 94-142 adds two other situations: (a) when a parent requests evaluation, and (b) when environmental or social conditions warrant evaluation.

What Conditions?

In two recent cases, *P-1 v. Shedd* (3 EHLR 551:164 [D. Conn. 1979]) and *Mattie T. v. Holladay* (3 EHLR 551:109 [D. Miss. 1979]), the condition warranting more evaluation was student misbehavior serious enough to call for expulsion. In two other recent cases, *Howard S. v. Friendswood* (454 F. Supp. 634 [S.D. Tex. 1978]) and *Stuart v. Nappi* (443 F. Supp. 1235 [D. Conn. 1978]), the federal courts suggested that persistent truancy from a supposedly appropriate special education program warranted a closer look at the child. Deciding what conditions warrant evaluation and reevaluation in a school district should be a priority for assessment personnel.

What Is Evaluated?

Every area of suspected disability must be examined, but evaluation is justified only if there is reason to suspect a problem. Federal law recognizes that the act of testing can itself be stigmatizing. Furthermore, the concept of using the least drastic means of evaluation (familiar to school personnel in choosing placement options as the least restrictive alternative) requires that only as much testing be used as is needed. The diagnostic inquiry clearly must not be limited by the evaluator's prejudgment of what is available prescriptively. For example, a hearing impaired child should be assessed for aural and oral ability even when the school currently offers only manual instruction through sign language and finger spelling. The diagnostic process must not change to accommodate programs the school chooses to make available; rather, the programs must accommodate the needs of the child as shown in an honest, comprehensive assessment.

Who Conducts the Evaluation?

The effort must be a multidisciplinary one, with an evaluator who is knowledgeable about each suspected area of disability. The multidisciplinary nature of the process is reaffirmed in the placement decision making, which must be based on information from a variety of sources and made by a group of people.

What Is Used for Evaluation?

Larry P. clarifies that a variety of information, ranging from formal tests to teacher observation, must be used. Regulations under both Section 504 and PL 94-142 specify the concern of Congress that whatever evaluation materials are used should not discriminate on the basis of irrelevant criteria (e.g., race or sex). *Larry P.* concerned racial and cultural bias, but the real challenge today is bias on the basis of handicap. Test manufac-

16

turers do not currently seem to be helping evaluators meet this challenge. For the next few years evaluators will have to approach their education agency to determine how to deal with tests that do not reasonably accommodate the needs of the handicapped.

What Is Produced by Evaluation?

Courts are beginning to recognize that a full evaluation produces not only diagnostic data but also information useful for the development of a prescription. Some schools disagree, viewing the prescription process as the province of the IEP meeting. Other districts forbid evaluators to write prescriptions, fearing the district would be bound to recommendations as stated in prescriptions. The district is only bound by the shared decisions in IEP meetings. The decision is a group-determined program based on individual evaluation data available to the team. In one recent case, *Winfield v. Fairfax County Board* (3 EHLR 551:269 [Cir. Ct. Fairfax Co., Va., 1979]), the court ordered an evaluator to write a prescription. The court held that a diagnosis alone did not meet the requirement for evaluation under PL 94-142.

One regulation overlooked by many districts involves a special written report as a product of any inquiry into a sus-

Courts are beginning to recognize that a full evaluation produces not only diagnostic data but also information useful for the development of a pre-scription.

pected learning disability. When the bulk of the regulations under PL 94-142 were promulgated, the formula for determining a learning disability was still being debated. The final decision was published in a separate set of regulations unknown to many districts. These regulations require written reports when children are assessed for learning disabilities. Team members must sign and indicate their agreement with the group conclusion. If members dissent, they must state their dissension in writing.

What Is the Parents' Role?

Parents, being the child's primary caretakers, have information useful to the evaluation process. A complete evaluation must document contact with parents and information received from them. The proposed program for the child must be communicated to the parents in a written statement. The notice must include a description of each evaluation procedure, test, record, or report the agency uses as a basis for the proposal, and it must be written in language understandable to the general public. Thus parents will be a source of information and will participate in programming decisions based on the evaluation data.

INDEPENDENT EVALUATIONS

Schools no longer "own" the evaluation process. An outside source, known as an independent evaluator, may be brought into the process. Congress, recognizing that schools often make mistakes, established as a check and balance the right of parents to have an independent evaluation. Although that right was established in PL 93-380, it was not clarified until regulations were promulgated under PL 94-142.

The sole definition of "independent evaluator" is that the person not be employed by the agency responsible for the education of the child in question. The parent then has the right to have the results of the evaluation considered with respect to decisions regarding a free, appropriate public education. The challenge for evaluators is not only that they might face an independent evaluator at an IEP meeting or impartial hearing but also that they themselves might be an independent evaluator in another district.

Parents' Rights

When parents procure the independent evaluation, they have a right to study the data and decide whether to share them with the school. The procedure is often misunderstood by school personnel, who must always share evaluation information without regard to whether the data affirm the school's position. One problem with parent-procured evaluations is that the independent evaluator may use tests or gather data in a manner unlike that required by the state. The statute and regulations make clear that even in such a case the school must consider the data in any decision made with respect to the provision of a free appropriate public education.

Parents also have the right to obtain the independent evaluation at public expense. If done at public expense, two conditions apply: (1) the independent evaluator must be a "qualified examiner" meeting the same qualifications as those imposed on the agency for a similar evaluation and (2) both the location of the testing and the criteria for testing must meet agency standards. An independent evaluation at public expense can be obtained in three ways. First, parents can ask the agency to procure one. Second, an impartial hearing officer might, of his or her own volition or at the parents' request, order an independent evaluation at public expense. Third, parents can obtain one on their own.

When a parent asks, the school must provide information about where the parent can acquire an independent educational evaluation. If parents believe the school's initial evaluation was inappropriate, they may send the bill for the independent evaluation to the school (which must pay the bill or initiate a due-process hearing and show that the school's evaluation was appropriate). Even if the school proves that its evaluation is appropriate (and the parents pay the bill), the independent evaluation must still be considered in the school's decision making.

When Evaluations Clash

Thus an evaluator might find himself or herself in an impartial hearing defending the appropriateness of his or her effort. The test of the evaluator will include, at a minimum, his or her compliance with all state and federal guidelines; and it might extend, at a maximum, to the quality of the diagnosis and prescription in comparison with that of the independent evalua-

18

tion. If there is a discrepancy between the type of disability identified by the school and that identified by the independent evaluator, the appropriateness of the school's evaluation would be in question. Another problem may occur if the school's and independent evaluator's evaluations disagree, however slightly, about the degree of disability and, subsequently, the type of service delivery that is most appropriate. In that case the decision as to the "appropriate" evaluation would be the decision of the hearing officer.

Emergency Discipline Judgments

A new role awaits evaluators in cases where "discipline" of the handicapped student is judged necessary. In *Stuart v. Nappi* and *S-1 v. Turlington* (3 EHLR 551:221 [S.D. Fla. 1979]) the courts considered the expulsion of handicapped students. In *Stuart* the Connecticut court held that expulsion would be a change in placement. In *S-1* the Florida court held that prior to expulsion a determination must be made whether the offending behavior was related to the handicapping condition. In either case, the court required the reconvening of the evaluation personnel to determine whether the misbehavior warranted further evaluation or if it indicated that services should be carried out in a different placement. Both cases make it clear that PL 94-142 supersedes local board policies on discipline. Thus the evaluators will be deciding the student's placement when previously the school board would have met to contend with the child.

It is a role many school board members will dislike. Many evaluators also will not welcome the added responsibility. If the misbehavior were so outrageous that there was pressure to work with the child immediately, then time for the evaluation would be very limited.

One case mentioned earlier, *P-1 v. Shedd,* creates a role for special education evaluators to assess a student, not identified as handicapped, who commits an act that warrants a recommendation for expulsion or suspension totaling more than 15 days in any school year. In such a case the child would be referred to an identification team to determine if the child is indeed handicapped. The special education process (IEP and placement) takes place in lieu of the established discipline process.

TESTIMONY AT TRIAL

One final role awaits evaluators. The new federal laws create a forum, the impartial due-process hearing, which is conducted in many states like a minitrial. These laws authorize parents to go to court to redress grievances. Evaluation personnel should become aware of the possibility of their being called to testify. Most evaluators with whom the author has discussed this prospect say they are ready and will simply tell their story. But the trial forum does not work that easily. If the questions directed toward the witness are poor, so is the witness.

Would it not be tragic to play the other roles of the evaluator properly but fail in this last role, resulting in an unjust placement for a child? The final role for evaluators is to work with school district personnel or school district legal counsel or enable them to understand how to use evaluators effectively as witnesses.

CONCLUSION

Evaluators have a variety of roles. Their diagnostic efforts must be comprehensive, open to parents, and merged into a multidisciplinary process. They must be prepared to respond to the challenge of an independent evaluation conducted by someone else or even to be an independent evaluator themselves. They must share the prescription process with parents and other education personnel in the IEP meeting. Finally, they must be ready to express their opinions in an emergency disciplinary session or in the artificial forum of a trial. Handicapped children will need their best efforts.

General Assessment Competencies for Special Education Teachers

Gaye McNutt
Linda Higbee Mandelbaum
University of Oklahoma
Norman, Oklahoma

REGARDLESS OF AGE, grade level, or educational placement of students, or of the subject matter being taught, educators who work with handicapped students periodically engage in assessment activities. The purposes of the assessment, the particular techniques used, and the amount of time expended may vary; but the success of any assessment effort depends on the competence of those individuals involved.

Competency statements for particular groups have been delineated by both individual authors and committees of professional organizations. Several lists of competencies have been published within the last few years. For example, the Division for Children with Learning Disabilities (1978) developed an extensive list of competencies for teachers of the learning disabled and is now collecting data related to them. Cegelka (1978) focused on competencies for persons responsible for the mentally retarded, and

0190-6900/80/0013-0021$2.00

the International Reading Association (1978) proposed a list of guidelines for reading teachers. Many universities and colleges also have developed assessment competencies keyed to their specific training programs. In some cases, these competency lists have been designed for only one type of teacher (e.g., teachers of the learning disabled) and usually for teachers who work at one particular age level.

The purpose of this article is to suggest areas of competence that would be useful for teachers of any type of handicapped students and for teachers of any age level of students. More specifically our purposes are (a) to briefly review four major knowledge areas that are prerequisite to the assessment competencies, (b) to propose a set of general assessment competencies that all special educators should acquire, regardless of educational philosophy, and (c) to outline implications and future directions that may result from these prerequisites and competencies. A definition of assessment is needed to clarify the purposes and our discussion related to them.

While there are many definitions of *assessment*, we have chosen to focus only on assessment activities that are used by teachers to acquire information concerning students' instructional needs. This definition is, admittedly, narrow in scope, because other types of assessment (e.g., assessment to identify students according to handicapping labels or assessment to evaluate the effectiveness of a program) are not included. However, assessing students to determine their instructional needs is a task *all* teachers normally

undertake, while other types of assessment are not used by all teachers. Additionally, many of the competencies that are related to assessing for instructional purposes are useful when assessment is used for other purposes.

PREREQUISITES

Before assessing students, educators should have a well-formed understanding of (a) educational philosophy, (b) educational goals, (c) child and adolescent development, (d) subject matter content, and (e) terminology. At least a minimal level of proficiency in these is essential before educators can consider the assessment competencies.

Educational Philosophy

An educational philosophy is a theoretical approach to education that an individual gradually develops. This philosophy includes beliefs related to how students learn and how they should be taught. Once a basic educational philosophy is developed, the specifics (e.g., choosing various methods or materials) become easier primarily because each is first judged in terms of whether it adheres to one's philosophy. The educational phi-

---

Before assessing students, educators should have a well-formed understanding of (a) educational philosophy, (b) educational goals, (c) child and adolescent development, (d) subject matter content, and (e) terminology.

---

losophy held by an individual helps ensure that all educationally related decisions are theoretically consistent with one another.

While many philosophies exist today, they are constantly changing. Some are gaining adherents and becoming stronger; others, ebbing. The philosophies prevalent among special educators today can be grouped into three broad categories: (a) ability training, (b) atomistic education, and (c) holistic education. Following is a brief discussion of each, based on an unpublished paper (Hammill, Brown, Brown, Gray, Hresko, Larsen, McNutt, Poplin, Reid, & Wiederholt, 1979) and a recent speech (Hammill, 1979).

ABILITY TRAINING

Essentially ability training assumes that certain presumed mental functions or psychological processes within the brain must be intact before individuals can efficiently learn specific educational content (e.g., reading or writing). If these abilities are not intact, the assumption is made that the weaknesses or problem areas can first be identified and then remediated or circumvented. Therefore application of this philosophy generally focuses on assessing and training basic mental processes or abilities such as attention, auditory or visual discrimination, memory, closure, sequencing, and ocular pursuit.

The various theories related to this basic philosophy are many and can be traced to ancient times. However, the educational application of this philosophy did not become dominant in special edu-

cation until the 1960s. Tests and materials by individuals such as Frostig, Getman, Kephart, and Kirk are examples of its application in special education. Research has generally failed to substantiate the usefulness of the tests and materials resulting from this orientation (Arter & Jenkins, 1979; Hammill & Larsen, 1974; Larsen & Hammill, 1975).

ATOMISTIC EDUCATION

Atomistic education basically assumes that (a) whatever is to be learned can be broken into discrete and independent segments or components, (b) the segments can be put into an orderly sequence, (c) these individual segments and rules can be taught, and (d) the learner will generalize these into a usable whole (i.e., the whole equals the sum of the parts). The various theories within this philosophy can be identified in the works of Pavlov, Thorndike, and others; but their application in special education was not strongly evident until the late 1960s and the 1970s. Application of this philosophy results in completing task analyses, creating scope and sequence charts, using behavioral objectives, and so on.

HOLISTIC EDUCATION

The holistic philosophy is based on three general assumptions. First is that the whole is different from the sum of its parts, and therefore teaching discrete segments (e.g., particular phonic skills in reading) will not necessarily result in learning being successful at the more general task (e.g., comprehending what is read). Second, learners can construct and verify their own rules (e.g., the rules young children possess but cannot state when learning to speak). Third, when teaching any task, that task must maintain the characteristics of the general content to which it belongs (e.g., reading tasks should require comprehension in meaningful context). Individuals such as Vygotsky, Piaget, Bruner, and Chomsky have presented theories related to this philosophy, but it is only beginning to influence special education in terms of practical application.

Educational Goals

Long-term educational goals should focus on the possibilities that exist for students after they complete the traditional 12 years of schooling, and enter the working world, sheltered employment, and so on. The important point related to this prerequisite is that teachers must consider what they are teaching and assessing in terms of its relationship to and effect upon the long-term goals. Tasks having little relationship to or effect on these goals should be seriously questioned in terms of their validity for being included in the curriculum.

Educators should develop a general perspective concerning (a) possible long-term educational goals and learning requirements related to obtaining each goal, (b) curricula that would result from attempting to reach the various goals, and (c) which goals are most important for the majority of the involved students. Maintaining flexibility in applying these goals to individual students is also important.

Child and Adolescent Development

Educators need a general knowledge of child and adolescent development to determine expectations for students and to decide when to assess these expectations. For example, a general knowledge of child and adolescent development enables teachers to set and assess reasonable expectations related to the attention span of the students, their ability to interact with one another, and other social and emotional variables.

Subject Matter Content

Whether the area to be assessed is academic (e.g., math, reading) or nonacademic (e.g., independent living skills), a thorough knowledge of that area is needed. For example, if mathematics will be assessed, the educator needs a basic understanding of number theory, computational processes, measurement, problem solving, and so on. Naturally, individuals' educational philosophies as well as their knowledge of child and adolescent development will influence the knowledge they gain in the content area.

Terminology

When professionals discuss the problems a student is having, difficulties often arise when different terms are used to describe the same problem or when the same term is used to describe different problems. For example, one teacher may define *dyslexia* as a problem of reversing letters in words; another may think of it as a difficulty in comprehending what is read; and yet another may define it as existing when words or entire lines are skipped during oral reading.

How individuals define various terms obviously affects their communication with one another and the assessment procedures that will be undertaken. Because the trends in special education appear to be toward mainstreaming, increasing interdisciplinary work, and using teams of professionals with each student, the ability to precisely define terminology and to recognize that a variety of definitions may exist for a single term is necessary if assessment and subsequent remediation procedures are to be effective.

Each of these prerequisites influences what will be assessed, how the assessment will proceed, and how the information will be used. These prerequisites also influence the actual instructional process.

GENERAL ASSESSMENT COMPETENCIES

The assessment competencies are presented as global statements so that they may be adapted by teachers of various age levels or types of handicapped students. Additionally, we present global statements because highly structured competencies represent only a particular philosophy and are difficult to incorporate into other philosophies. (See Blackhurst, 1977, for a model of how more specific competencies lead to behavioral objectives and curriculum development.)

The competencies are grouped into three categories: (a) techniques, (b) application, and (c) synthesis. The first category is factual information that all teachers should possess regardless of their philosophy, educational goals for students, or other prerequisites. As a rule, attaining skill in these techniques is not greatly influenced by the opinions and positions that result from the prerequisites. However, the latter two categories (i.e., application of the techniques and synthesis of the resulting information) are influenced by the opinions and positions that result from the prerequisites.

Techniques

All assessment data can be organized and obtained through one of three basic techniques: (a) analysis of a product, (b) interviewing, or (c) observation. Although each technique may be applied in many ways and contributes particular types of assessment information, there is some overlap in terms of the various procedures within each of the three categories.

ANALYSIS OF A PRODUCT

Analysis of a product is examining work completed by an individual. For example, when teachers score and interpret tests, grade essays, or check homework assignments, they are analyzing products.

Educators need to understand the differences among three types of tests and should be skilled in four knowledge areas related to each. The types of tests are norm-referenced, criterion-referenced,

All assessment data can be organized and obtained through one of three basic techniques: (a) analysis of a product, (b) interviewing, or (c) observation.

and informal; the knowledge areas are test selection, construction, administration, and interpretation.

According to Gronlund (1976), norm-referenced tests allow a student's results to be compared with some known group's performance (the norming sample). Because norm-referenced tests have a highly quantitative nature, they are not particularly useful in assessing for instructional planning. Criterion-referenced testing is more qualitative. It compares the individual's performance with a specified content domain (Anastasi, 1976). Informal tests are usually teacher-made and may be in the form of short-answer objective tests or more subjective written tests (Wallace & Larsen, 1978). Educators should possess skills in each of the following knowledge areas as they apply to the three kinds of tests:

1. Test selection focuses on determining which type of test is more appropriate and choosing particular tests within one of the categories. Skill in making judgments about reliability, validity, norming samples, what test results to expect, and so on are necessary for proficient test selection. Mastery of the other knowledge areas related to tests is also necessary.

2. Test construction is most useful in creating criterion-referenced and informal instruments. Although most teachers are not involved in constructing norm-referenced tests, knowledge related to their construction is helpful when selecting such tests. Some of the basic information about construction of tests includes how to create a pool of items and eliminate inadequate ones, determining and improving reliability and validity when pos-

sible, and delineating administration and scoring procedures.

3. Competency in test administration includes not only how to appropriately administer various tests but also how to judge if a test was properly administered when given by another individual. Naturally, the results from improperly administered tests must be viewed as possibly inaccurate or misleading.

4. Proficiency in interpreting test results should be obtained only after other knowledge areas related to tests have been mastered. The interpretation and subsequent application of the results affect the instructional planning for individual students, which is a major reason for undertaking assessment procedures.

Tests are only one of the products that can be analyzed. Analyzing classwork or homework for patterns or types of errors (e.g., failure to use semicolons appropriately) is included in this area, as is analyzing work for particular strengths. Other products to analyze may be creative acts or their results (e.g., art work or music). Educators may also analyze past records of the student. In general, competency in analysis of products other than tests is closely related to mastery of informal testing and proficiency in the prerequisites of content knowledge as well as child and adolescent development.

INTERVIEWING

While interviewing is one way to gather assessment information, skillful use of its techniques enhances the cooperation of all those concerned with a student. Closely related to these skills is the general ability to get along well with people.

Following are examples of interviewing competencies:

- Asking specific questions that are easy to understand and that will provide the needed information.
- Questioning in an informal manner so that the interviewee does not become defensive.
- Listening and responding appropriately to the answers and questions of others.
- Making note of or remembering pertinent information.

OBSERVATION

Observing provides educators with information not obtainable in other ways. For example, interaction between the regular classroom teacher and the student can be determined through observation, because either the student or the teacher, or both, may view the situation differently. The following are some of the competencies needed for effective observation:

- Being inconspicuous or unobtrusive when observing. Generally, an outsider must visit a classroom several times before students become accustomed to his or her presence. This is particularly important because the behavior of students is often different when an outsider is present.
- Selecting the appropriate behavior(s) to be observed and identifying other relevant behaviors that may affect the one selected.
- Using appropriate recording or measuring devices for the observation of behavior. These may be highly

structured or, at the other extreme, they may rely only on clinical judgment or insight.
- Being objective.

In attaining these general competencies, individuals with an atomistic philosophy might use Hall's (1974) or others' techniques for applied behavior analysis. Individuals adhering to a holistic philosophy might rely on the section entitled "Analysis of the Learner in the Classroom" that appears in *The Resource Teacher* (Wiederholt, Hammill, & Brown, 1978).

Application

Before determining which of the basic techniques to use and actually gathering the information, special education teachers must be able to make decisions related to the following questions.

- What area is going to be assessed (e.g., reading, social interactions, math)? Aspects of the area to be assessed should be as specific as possible and will likely be influenced by the individual's educational philosophy, knowledge of the content, and knowledge of child and adolescent development. For example, individuals with an atomistic educational philosophy might consider assessing phonics skills, sound blending, or structural analysis within reading. In contrast, individuals with a holistic educational philosophy might focus on comprehension abilities when different types of reading materials (e.g., newspapers, recipes, history tests) are used.

28

- What types of information are needed? Student performance on actual tasks is usually gathered. Other types of information might focus on attitudes and expectations held by the student or his or her parents.
- Which individuals should be included in the assessment? The assessment process usually focuses on the student. However, assessment information can also be gathered from teachers and other professionals, the student's peers, and the parents.

By making these decisions and applying them to the techniques of assessment, special educators should be ready to actually gather the assessment data. In some instances, other individuals may also assist in gathering the data (e.g., when information is gathered to write an individualized education program).

Synthesis

Synthesis is probably the most crucial of the three assessment categories and is highly dependent on the previous two. Despite its importance, it is seldom mentioned in competency statements or textbooks for special education teachers.

Proficiency in this category means the ability to take all of the previously gathered assessment information and combine the separate data and ideas to form a cohesive whole. This then becomes the basis for instructional programming. Following are some of the skills that may be required to accomplish this:

- Separating information that appears to be accurate from that which may need verifying.

- Determining if conflicting assessment information is present; if so, deciding which information should be considered more accurate and finding why the discrepancy exists.
- Eliminating information that is redundant or not useful for instructional planning.
- Comparing the information to draw up an order of importance for remedial action.

IMPLICATIONS AND FUTURE DIRECTIONS

This article is an initial attempt to consolidate and add to currently available competency statements so that they can have broader applications. We have attempted to state a general order (i.e., prerequisites followed by assessment competencies), broaden the competencies to include any type of special education teacher, and to avoid highly structured statements that lock individuals into a particular educational philosophy. On the basis of these initial competencies, there are three major implications to consider.

First, the competencies presented here focus only on assessment for instructional purposes. We hope that a comprehensive set of competencies will be developed in the future and that relevant data will be gathered. If all special education programs related their specific competencies to a general set, contrasting particular programs would be easier. This would also enable individuals to choose the program that seemed best suited to their own needs and beliefs.

Second, individuals may wish to take these initial competencies and judge their own abilities relative to them. If they detect weaknesses, they may wish to pursue further study. Such study might take the form of attending university classes, reading independently, or attending relevant conferences.

Finally, a variety of special education organizations and other professional organizations have alluded to national credentialing of special educators in the future. However, each organization may have different beliefs related to competencies required for credentialing teachers. Therefore developing a set of general competencies may serve as a framework for initial communication.

REFERENCES

Anastasi, A. *Psychological testing* (4th ed.). New York: Macmillan, 1976.

Arter, J. A., & Jenkins, J. R. Differential diagnosis-prescriptive teaching: A critical appraisal. *Review of Educational Research,* 1979, *49,* 517-555.

Blackhurst, A. E. Competency-based special education personnel preparation. In R. D. Kneedler & S. G. Tarver (Eds.), *Changing perspectives in special education.* Columbus, Ohio: Charles E. Merrill, 1977.

Cegelka, W. J. Competencies of persons responsible for the classification of mentally retarded individuals. *Exceptional Children,* 1978, *45,* 26-31.

Division for Children with Learning Disabilities. *Competencies for teachers of learning disabled children and youth.* Reston, Va.: DCLD, 1978.

Gronlund, N. E. *Measurement and evaluation in teaching* (3rd ed.). New York: Macmillan, 1976.

Hall, R. V. *Behavior modification: The measurement of behavior* (rev. ed.). Lawrence, Kan.: H & H Enterprises, 1974.

Hammill, D. *The field of learning disabilities: A futuristic perspective.* Speech given at the National Conference on Learning Disabilities, Louisville, Ky., October, 1979.

Hammill, D. D., Brown, L., Brown, V., Gray, R., Hresko, W., Larsen, S.C., McNutt, G., Poplin, M.S., Reid, D. K., & Wiederholt, J. L. *A model for classifying instructional strategies.* Unpublished manuscript, 1979. (7701 Cameron Road; Austin, Tex. 78752.)

Hammill, D., & Larsen, S. C. The relationship of selected auditory perceptual skills to reading ability. *Journal of Learning Disabilities,* 1974, *1,* 429-436.

International Reading Association. *Guidelines for the professional preparation of reading teachers.* Newark, Del.: author, 1978.

Larsen, S. C., & Hammill, D. D. Relationship of selected visual perceptual abilities to school learning. *Journal of Special Education,* 1975, *9,* 281-291.

Wallace, G., & Larsen, S. C. *Educational assessment of learning problems: Testing for teaching.* Boston: Allyn & Bacon, 1978.

Wiederholt, J. L., Hammill, D. D., & Brown, V. *The resource teacher: A guide to effective practices.* Boston: Allyn & Bacon, 1978.

Nonbiased Assessment of Minority Group Children

Thomas Oakland
The University of Texas
Austin, Texas

THE NEED TO KNOW and to fully understand pupils is one of the strongest tenets of the educational profession. Educators also believe that knowledge of pupils is increased by acquiring information through various assessment techniques. Formal and informal methods have been developed that enable educators to describe and evaluate children's academic, intellectual, perceptual, linguistic, social, and emotional characteristics. Assessment has become a cornerstone of the profession.

Educators also know assessment techniques have their limitations. For example, tests have been criticized because they may rigidly shape school curricula and restrict educational change, promote a view that human abilities are fixed and unmodifiable, foster undesirable biases and expectations, invade a person's privacy, and imperfectly predict future behaviors (Cronbach, 1975; Holmen & Docter, 1972; Oakland, 1974).

0106 6060/80/0013 0031$2.00

Tests have always been criticized. However, during the last decade, critics have become more vocal, adamant, and numerous—particularly among blacks, Hispanics, and other racial and ethnic minorities (Samuda, 1975). Critics have demonstrated how tests denigrate minority persons' dignity and pride, restrict educational and vocational opportunities, serve to dehumanize and institutionalize decision-making practices, and maintain prejudicial attitudes (Oakland, 1973).

This article examines issues regarding the assessment of minority group children from three perspectives. The first section reviews potential problems that impede attempts to develop suitable psychoeducational programs for minority group children. The second section looks specifically at points before, during, and after assessment that may bias assessment. The third section presents suggestions for providing nonbiased programs.

A BROAD VIEW OF POTENTIAL PROBLEMS

Discussions of nonbiased assessment tend to focus on tests and testing. One often concludes, after considering limited information, that tests are bad.

This categorical position is incorrect. It also helps to perpetuate a set of attitudes that impede the development of appropriate diagnostic-intervention techniques for minority group children. To be effective, educators who use these techniques must consider a number of potential problems that arise in working with children generally and with minority group children in particular.

Children

Children who are uncooperative and poorly motivated, who devalue education, are unable to take tests, and exhibit obstreperous behaviors impede educators' ability to acquire a complete and accurate assessment of what they can and cannot do.

Parents

Parents may know a Monday night television schedule more thoroughly than their children's daily schedule. Others are caught up in the "me" generation and lack a proper sense of dedication to their children. Some are unable to make objective, intelligent decisions regarding their children's welfare. They may be uncooperative, apprehensive, and afraid of the school. They may not have time—or know how—to help. Various values of the home may be inconsistent with those of the school. For example, parents may encourage children to remain at home to do chores or to get a part-time job (which often escalates to a full-time job). Families may move frequently. Some urban schools experience a 100% student turnover rate yearly.

Examiners

Some examiners are poorly trained. They lack knowledge of minority groups, rigidly approach each case in the same repetitive way, and seek shortcuts to complicated situations.

Assessment Techniques

All assessment techniques may not be equally suited to children from different racial, ethnic, and cultural groups and for those families of lower socioeconomic status. Only by knowing a test's reliability and validity data, standardization sample, and other appropriate characteristics can educators know under what conditions a test can be used most confidently. Standardized tests are but one way to assess children. Other techniques include informal observations; interviews; class records and reports; criterion-referenced tests; behavioral assessment; reports from peers, teachers, parents, and other significant adults; anecdotal information; sociograms; questionnaires; and informal personality measures. Nonbiased assessment is achieved by choosing the most suitable techniques that help us acquire the information we want.

Educators

Teachers who want to rid their rooms of a particular child, refuse to try different educational and behavioral strategies, distort information, are uncooperative, and think that the children's environment is so deleterious that nothing they do will be beneficial also stand in the way of developing suitable programs.

Principals impede good programs when they provide insufficient support for special services; are uncomfortable working with children with special handicaps, those in minority groups, or those from families of low socioeconomic status; adopt dictatorial leadership styles rather than facilitative problem-solving styles;

and draw rigid boundaries between the school and the neighborhood, thus inhibiting teachers and parents from forming important and mutually supportive relationships regarding their children.

School Districts

School district policies often promote development of a bureaucratic network insensitive to the individual needs and characteristics of children, their families, and teachers. During the last 20 years the federal government has actively shaped school policies and programs through legislation and judicial decisions. In implementing school policies to comply with the law, educators may lose sight of their primary goal: to provide high-quality professional services to children and their families. School districts that identify many children for special education programs so that they ensure themselves their full share of state and federal funds are but one common example of this trend.

Many urban school districts are financially troubled, constantly facing the threat of strikes and other disruptions in their programs, and having a high turnover rate and low morale among professional staff and children. These problems exacerbate attempts to develop programs

---

In implementing school policies to comply with the law, educators may lose sight of their primary goal: to provide high-quality professional services to children and their families.

---

34   suitable for children who come from diverse racial, ethnic, cultural, and social class groups.

Isolated rural districts also have their limitations and problems. They, too, tend to lack financial resources and personnel and are tradition-bound; changes often occur slowly.

PL 94-142

The effect of PL 94-142 has been significant and far reaching on education generally and on nonbiased assessment specifically (see, in this issue, Martin, pp. 13-19). One effect has been to encourage school psychologists to assess more children directly and to not provide consultation services to teachers, principals, and parents. This has resulted in dramatically increasing the number of children being referred for appraisal. Through their consulting activities, school psychologists and other assessment specialists often are able to work directly with teachers and parents to arrive at viable solutions to children's educational and psychological problems without doing a complete appraisal, thus permitting greater numbers of children to be seen.

Some legal requirements seem beyond the capabilities of school districts. Consider that the schools in New York and Chicago are responsible for assessing and teaching those children whose native language may be 1 of 200 languages and dialects. This obligation is not being—and probably cannot be—met. Clearly problems in assessing minority group children have no one source. They may be due to children; parents; examiners; assessment techniques; teachers; principals; district policies, practices, and financial abilities; and legal issues.

POSSIBLE BIAS POINTS

Educators and psychologists have direct control over only some of the conditions that directly influence nonbiased assessment, mainly situations occurring at school. Some of these conditions occur *prior* to assessment; others occur *during* assessment; still others occur *following* assessment.

Bias Points Prior to Assessment

REFERRAL AND SCREENING

The diagnostic-intervention process begins when a teacher refers a child for special services. Administrative procedures for processing referrals differ among districts. In some, children's names are put on a waiting list to be screened and evaluated. In other districts, names are referred to a within-school committee responsible for screening the referral after collecting existing data and obtaining additional information, including an appraisal of whether resources exist within the school to meet the children's needs.

The nature of the behaviors that actually stimulate the referral may constitute a bias point. Teachers may refer as academic problems those children who are not the lowest academically in class but whose behaviors they find disturbing. Other teachers have lower expectations for children who live in mobile homes, come from lower-class homes, attend unconventional churches, dress poorly, come from one-parent families, speak a foreign language, recently arrived in town, or have other distinguishable characteristics. A child's skin color or last name may stimulate other deep-seated prejudices. Prejudices may result in identifying qualities that are not present, encouraging the development of latent qualities, and overlooking other characteristics. For example, speech problems among children from bilingual backgrounds or those who speak nonstandard dialects often are overlooked. Health problems teachers readily detect among middle-class children may be unattended in lower-class children.

In New York City, over 90% of children referred for special services are found eligible for those services. Some districts may have even higher ratios of referred children to eligible children. An imbalance in the number of children from minority groups placed in special education begins at this point. Thus an examination of referral and screening procedures may indicate this to be a significant source of bias.

TEST NORMS

One assumption underlying assessment is that the child being tested could have been included in the test's standardization sample (i.e., the children whose scores constitute the test norms). The norms for many tests are large, heterogeneous, and well selected to adequately reflect the full range of children's characteristics. Others have a restricted and narrow standardization sample. No test is inherently biased. Bias enters when someone *uses* a test with an inappropriate standardization sample. Thus knowing a test's standardization samples is prerequisite for a nonbiased assessment program.

TEST RELIABILITY

Reliability refers to the stability of a person's performance. For test scores to be accurate, they must be stable. Although the reliability of test scores for majority- and minority-group children tend to be similar, school districts should conduct their own studies to decide the degree of confidence they can have in their test data. One also should keep in mind that objectively acquired data from formal measures (e.g., from standardized achievement and intelligence tests) tend to be more reliable than data from informal and less objective techniques (e.g., class grades, behavior observation, and teacher reports). Designing nonbiased programs requires the selection and use of reliable data-gathering techniques.

TEST VALIDITY

Valid measures accurately assess behaviors they are designed to measure. When measures are valid, accurate decisions are made and the results used with confidence; when they do not, inaccurate decisions flourish. Thus the degree of confidence educators can have in using measures is contingent on knowing this information. No test is accurate for all purposes. Tests are selected for specific reasons and to provide accurate information to specific questions.

36

While the prevailing data suggest that intelligence test validity is similar for majority and minority children (Jensen, 1980), other studies suggest this is not always the case. For example, one study (Oakland, 1978) reports the ability of the Metropolitan Readiness Test to predict Metropolitan Achievement Test scores 2 years later to be .77% for whites, .30% for Mexican-Americans, and .15% for blacks. This should not be interpreted as an indictment of all tests. Local, regional, and statewide studies are needed to ascertain the validity of tests used with minority group children. Only by knowing the validity of the data can a program be certified as nonbiased.

Bias Points During Assessment

Characteristics that can lead to bias during the assessment include child characteristics, examiner characteristics, and the adequacy of diagnostic-intervention techniques.

CHILD CHARACTERISTICS

Language. Children's ability to understand and communicate in English is very important. School success partly depends on the ability to understand, speak, read, and write English. Knowing children's listening and speaking proficiency in English is important in judging whether their language skills are sufficiently developed to enable them to take other tests adequately.

Conventional measures requiring a high level of English proficiency cannot be used with children whose English language skills are poorly developed. Paucity

Conventional measures requiring a high level of English proficiency cannot be used with children whose English language skills are poorly developed.

of language might be due to general language deficiencies among English-speaking children or to language differences due to either the child's exposure to nonstandard dialects or to the child's exclusive knowledge of a language other than English. Tests used in schools generally are not intended to directly assess language skills but use language to assess intelligence, achievement, personality, and other characteristics. In working with children with language differences, educators need to alter their conventional assessment techniques to obtain a valid picture of intellectual, personality, and social characteristics.

Test wiseness. In giving tests, educators assume that children possess certain abilities prerequisite to taking tests. For example, they assume that children can understand the directions (which might include concepts such as right, left, up, down, same, and different), that children will consider all possible responses before choosing an answer, that children can work on one item at a time and not be distracted by other items, and that children are involved and attentive during the full test. These and other abilities (Oakland, 1972) constitute basic test-taking skills. Children must have these prerequisite skills for tests to be valid (see, in this issue, Reid & Hresko, pp. 47-57).

Motivation and anxiety. Adequate test performance requires that children be properly motivated (Oakland & Matuszek, 1977). Too often, children randomly select answers on a multiple-choice test or refuse to cooperate in other ways. Other children may be extremely anxious and unable to attend to the test. A nonbiased assessment program must consider the attitudinal characteristics of children to ensure that they are properly motivated. Results from aptitude and achievement tests are valid only when children are fully motivated to try to do their very best work.

Cultural differences. Minority children often come from restricted environments or from cultural settings that provide opportunities for growth and development differing significantly from those of most children (Cole & Bruner, 1971; Newland, 1973). These differences may be seen in child-rearing practices, expectations and aspirations, language experiences, informal and formal learning experiences, and other factors that constitute acculturation patterns. The acculturation patterns of minority group children and those from lower socioeconomic homes may be significantly different from acculturation patterns of children included in a test's standardization sample. Confidence in a test decreases when a child's acculturation patterns with respect to the characteristics being assessed are judged to be significantly different from those of the standardization sample.

Not all children from minority or lower socioeconomic status groups differ significantly from children included in the standardization sample. The decision on whether a child's acculturation patterns are similar to those of other children must be made for each child *individually* and can be made competently only with thorough knowledge of each child's background and knowledge of the test's standardization sample.

Expectations. Individuals' behavior tends to move toward the expectations others hold of them. When children are expected to be well behaved and these expectations are communicated to them, the prevalence of good behavior increases. Children tend to adopt and accept the expectations their peers, family, and teachers communicate to them. Knowing a child's expectations enables educators to more accurately appraise the child's future and to alter their interpretations of the assessment data. A child who expects to fail on tests is likely to underperform on tests. Thus low expectations tend to exacerbate other problems and decrease the validity of test data.

EXAMINER CHARACTERISTICS

The assessment specialist plays a central role in designing and implementing a nonbiased assessment program. Three particular areas serve as guides.

Bias attitudes. Teachers' attitudes toward children affect their behavior toward children. Teachers who feel attachment and concern toward students behave differently from those who feel rejection or indifference toward students. Moreover, teachers' attitudes are directly affected by children's characteristics. Educators generally tend to favor bright, achieving, linguistically competent, academically motivated, compliant, conforming stu-

38

dents. But many children being referred for assessment exhibit different characteristics. Furthermore, some persons have strong and fixed opinions regarding persons of identifiable racial, ethnic, and social class groups. These prejudices act as roadblocks that prevent persons from getting to know and understand the characteristics of each individual. Assessment specialists are not immune to these prejudices. They, too, may have their biases. Thus it is important to assess the extent to which bias may discolor and alter both the information acquired and the interpretations made of this information while working with persons of different racial or ethnic groups.

Who is the client? The Ethical Standards of Psychologists (American Psychological Association, 1972) emphasize the belief in the dignity and worth of the individual, a commitment to freedom of inquiry and communications, and a concern for the best interest of clients, colleagues, and society in general. Psychologists are strongly encouraged to respect the integrity and protect the welfare of persons with whom they work. When a conflict arises among professional workers, psychologists should be more concerned with the welfare of their clients (e.g., a child) than with the interest of their professional group.

However, this principle is not always adhered to. Some examiners are most concerned about job security, friendships, and serving the school system that employs them. Persons in this frame of mind will not fully investigate all school-related factors that may attenuate a child's performance. To find a deficit within the child and to fault the child's home and neighborhood often is easier than to identify important teacher and other school-related variables that are retarding the child's development. A nonbiased assessment of programs assumes that the examiner has an open mind and investigates both school- and home-related factors that may be hampering a child's development.

Competency. Examiners tend to be highly trained, competent, and dedicated. However, some know assessment superficially and mechanically. They are poorly prepared in child-clinical techniques and behavioral assessment and have not kept up with other advancements made in the field of appraisal. Many minority group parents and those with low incomes have come to depend on the public schools to provide good quality education and psychological services. These parents do not have the financial means to purchase these services privately. Thus the standards governing the provision of educational and psychological services in public schools must remain as high as those for the private sector. Nonbiased assessment is based on providing the highest quality of services to children and their families through public schools. Services short of this goal cannot be justified or tolerated.

ADEQUACY OF DIAGNOSTIC-INTERVENTION TECHNIQUES

Recently all assessment specialists in a large eastern school district were told to identify children for the resource room by administering 4 of 12 subtests from the Wechsler Intelligence Scale for Children, one figure drawing, and a visual-motor test. Fortunately, the assessment specialists recognized the gross inadequacies of this plan and refused to comply with the directive. Specialists should not be called on to make important decisions based on meager information derived from short-cut strategies. They need multiple kinds of information. They need information about the medical, social, psychological, and educational characteristics of children. Because the human being is a complex organism, problems in one or more of these areas affect development in other areas. Thus one strong focus must include multiple kinds of information on children's characteristics (see memorandum from the Office for Civil Rights, in Oakland, 1973).

Home and school factors that may be contributing to the child's problems also need to be understood. This requires an ecological focus in which educators examine interrelationships among child, home, and school. Rarely is there one single cause for significant school problems. Usually many factors either cause or support dysfunctional school behavior. To be complete, nonbiased assessment must consider a variety of school and home factors in addition to children's characteristics.

Bias Points After Assessment

Assessment is a process—not a goal. It provides ways to collect and interpret information relevant to making decisions. The goal within education is to make wise and informed decisions that will benefit the child educationally, psychologically,

and socially. Thus the effectiveness of our nonbiased assessment program hinges on what happens to the child following assessment. Three principal barriers must be removed to have a proper program following assessment.

NO INTERVENTION

The fundamental principle underlying a nonbiased assessment program is that, if necessary, some attempt will be made to facilitate children's development. Yet in all too many situations, specialized interventions do not occur. While new labels may be placed on the child, resulting in a different class assignment, important and more effective curricular and behavioral strategies may not follow.

The diagnostic-intervention model put forth by Cromwell, Blashfield, and Strauss (1975) merges assessment information with interventions and thus helps to establish a standard for our practices. Four components of this model are described briefly.

The first component is concerned with acquiring historical information to assist educators in understanding a child and his or her environment. Information of a historical nature helps educators identify and understand important antecedent events in a child's life.

The second component seeks information that describes current characteristics of the child and his or her environment. Thus the first two components constitute a diagnostic side of the diagnostic-intervention strategy.

The third component focuses on interventions. Interventions include any process over which educators have control

40

and are developed from information gathered from the first two components.

A fourth component estimates the successfulness of the interventions. Given these previous and current characteristics, educators should be able to forecast the likelihood of a particular intervention's helpfulness to the child.

Thus a complete diagnostic-intervention program would acquire historical and current information on children and their environment. It would compare these two sources of information to draw associations between their previous and current characteristics. It would use this information to specify viable interventions and then would conduct follow-up studies to examine their effectiveness.

NO REEXAMINATION

The fourth component of this model provides for evaluating the effectiveness of interventions. This will require periodic review and reexamination of children to determine the extent to which progress is being made. With the goal of providing beneficial interventions, educators need to continuously update information and readjust interventions. Failure to reexamine children contributes a significant degree of bias.

DISPROPORTIONATE ASSIGNMENT TO INFERIOR EDUCATIONAL PROGRAMS

A third bias point is reached when large numbers of minority children are routinely placed in lower ability groups, educable mentally retarded classes, and other administrative structures judged to be ineffective and inferior to regular education programs (Laosa & Oakland, 1974).

A third bias point is reached when large numbers of minority children are routinely placed in lower ability groups, educable mentally retarded classes, and other structures judged to be inferior.

For example, blacks constituted 9% of California's population and 26% of the educable mentally retarded (EMR) population. Given the strong and pervasive notion that such classes are ineffective educational dead-ends, minority groups believe their disproportionate assignment to these classes provide prima facie evidence for discriminatory practices.

One Approach to Nonbiased Assessment: PL 94-142

Involvement of the federal government in education has mushroomed during the last 25 years, particularly after the *Brown v. Board of Education* decision. The government increased its involvement to protect the constitutional and statutory rights of minorities following the unwillingness or inability of states and local districts to alter allegedly discriminatory educational policies and practices.

The federal district courts considered allegations that educational programs for minorities are inferior, that schools discriminate against non-English-speaking students, that tests and assessment practices are biased, and that parents' rights are abrogated. By enacting PL 94-142 the government established uniform guidelines for schools to help overcome these and other problems.

While the scope of issues addressed by PL 94-142 is much broader than assessment and minority group children, the law has shaped nonbiased assessment practices more than any other source (Bateman & Herr, in press; Ysseldyke & Shinn, in press; and in this issue, Martin, pp. 13-19). As a federal law, it affects school districts in all 50 states and territories. All state education agencies have rewritten their policies and procedures to conform to this law. Principal features pertaining specifically to nonbiased assessment programs include the following rights.

RIGHT TO DUE PROCESS

Procedure safeguards guarantee the rights of parents to a meaningful role within the diagnostic-intervention process. The due process provisions include the right to examine all relevant records; to obtain an independent evaluation of the child; to receive written notices in their native language before the school district proposes to initiate a change or refuses to initiate the change in identifying, evaluating, or placing a child; the right to present complaints with respect to any matter relating to identifying, evaluating, or placing their child; the right to a hearing conducted by an impartial hearing officer employed by the state education agency; the right to appeal decisions to the state education agency; the right to be advised by legal counsel, to present evidence, to cross-examine witnesses, and to compel the attendance of witnesses; the right to a verbatim record of such hearings; the right to written findings of facts and deci-

sions; and the right to bring civil action in any state or district court of the United States.

RIGHT TO EDUCATION WITH NONHANDICAPPED CHILDREN

Handicapped children should be educated to the maximum extent possible with nonhandicapped children. Special classes, separate schools, and other administrative arrangements which move handicapped children from regular education should occur only when the nature and severity of the handicapped are not appropriately met through regular classes or the use of supplementary aids and services.

RIGHT TO TESTS THAT ARE NOT CULTURALLY DISCRIMINATORY

Tests will be selected and administered so as to not be racially or culturally discriminatory. Tests and other evaluation materials must be validated for the specific purpose for which they are used. Tests must be administered by trained personnel in accordance with the standardized instructions, in the child's native language, and for the specific purpose for which the tests were developed. When testing children with impaired sensory, manual, or speaking skills, tests must be selected and administered so as to accurately reflect the children's characteristics rather than their impairments. Finally, the evaluation must be directed to assess specific areas of educational need, not merely general constructs such as intelligence.

RIGHT TO A MULTIDIMENSIONAL, TEAM-BASED ASSESSMENT

Multiple kinds and sources of information should be acquired during the assessment (Gerry, 1973). The child is assessed in all areas relating to the suspected disability, including, whenever appropriate, health, vision, hearing, social and emotional status, general intelligence, academic performance, communicative status, and motor abilities. Information is also needed on the child's social and cultural background and adaptive behavior. In addition, information should be obtained from teachers, including their recommendations for the child.

Placement decisions must be made by groups of persons who are knowledgeable about the child, the evaluation data, and placement options. The evaluation made by a multidisciplinary team is a cornerstone to nonbiased assessment. An appropriate education program considers all data; no single procedure is used as the sole criterion for determining an appropriate educational program.

Periodic reevaluation of children receiving special education and related services must occur. Thus decisions must be regularly reviewed, with options open for each child to be maintained in special education or brought back into regular education.

Other Attempts to Achieve Nonbiased Assessment

Educators and psychologists have attempted to devise more appropriate psychoeducational assessment procedures for minority groups in various ways. Most techniques have focused on testing and examiners, some have focused on system changes, and a few have focused on changing children (Davis, 1974).

CHANGING TESTS

The development of culture-free tests during the 1940s and 1950s represented an attempt to find assessment techniques that could be used internationally and would not reflect cultural and socioeconomic differences. The strong influence a particular culture has on shaping behaviors is now widely realized. Cultures can differ dramatically in the behaviors they encourage people to develop. Thus the development of culture-free tests of important and meaningful characteristics in the behavioral sciences is not possible.

Culture-fair testing then became a goal (Eells, 1951; Jensen, 1970). A test is judged to be culture-fair if four conditions exist: (a) the mean scores and standard deviations for all racial, ethnic, and social-class groups within one country are the same, (b) persons from various racial, ethnic, and social class groups are included in the standardization sample, (c) the items minimize reading and language abilities, and (d) the test is untimed. Few tests meet these four conditions. For example, the mean scores on supposedly culture-fair tests tend to be lower for children from the lower social classes. Moreover, these tests often have low validity.

Culture-specific tests (Williams, 1971) also were seen as an answer. Tests were developed for a specific racial or ethnic group having a common identifiable cultural and geographic area. However, the scope of assessment is so large within the United States that this solution is impractical. There are not enough resources to develop culture-specific tests. Moreover, their reliability and validity are also questionable.

Criterion-referenced measures (Drew, 1973) also were described as an answer. By assessing the specific educational goals educators attempted to make testing more relevant to educational interventions. While criterion-referenced measures are helpful, they have a narrow scope and do not elicit reasons why children may be doing poorly in school.

The System of Multicultural Pluralistic Assessment (Mercer & Lewis, 1978) is one of the newer approaches to nonbiased assessment. It presents a more complete battery consisting of independent measures of children's medical, psychological, and social characteristics but does not consider information on children's educational achievement.

Translating tests from English into black dialects or foreign languages attempts to facilitate communication and make the tests more relevant linguistically. It is difficult to translate tests and yet maintain the integrity of the abilities being assessed. Moreover, there are no national linguistic standards for nonstandard dialects. An English-language test translated into Spanish for children in the Texas valley is inappropriate linguistically when used with Mexican-American children in California, Puerto Rican children in New York, and Cuban children in Miami.

An English-language test translated into Spanish for children in the Texas valley is inappropriate linguistically when used with Puerto Rican children in New York and Cuban children in Miami.

The development of racial and ethnic norms also was suggested as a means of implementing nonbiased assessment techniques. Tests could provide separate norms for blacks, Mexican-Americans, Indians, and children from other racial or ethnic groups. While most test standardization samples now include minority groups, their numbers are often too small to use as a basis for establishing separate norms. Moreover, presenting separate racial norms invites invidious comparisons.

Pluralistic norms and estimated learning potential (Mercer & Lewis, 1978), the upward adjustment of test scores earned by lower socioeconomic children so as to normalize mean score differences, have provoked much interest recently. However, pluralistic norms and the estimated learning potential presently lack conceptual clarity and empirical support (see *School Psychology Digest*, 1979, 8, 1 & 2).

Identification of item bias also has been tried (Green, no date; Jensen, 1975; Oakland & Feigenbaum, 1979, 1980). The statistical data currently are published on a few tests, and the results are not well known. Moreover, this line of investigation fails to deal with other professional, political, and social problems associated with the assessment of minority group children.

CHANGING EXAMINERS

Pairing examiners and children of the same race and language abilities has been used as a means to effect nonbiased assessment. Some people have assumed that performance of black children will be higher with black examiners and Mexican-American children with Mexican-American examiners. However, the evidence does not support this idea (Sattler, 1973). Interpersonal skills, rather than the racial characteristics of the examiner, appear to be more crucial in obtaining maximum performance from children.

Other examiner characteristics, such as the quality and recency of their training and their knowledge of minority group children and adults, have been discussed as an important component of nonbiased assessment. In-service training and continuing education continue to be used as a means of sensitizing and informing examiners to various issues pertinent to nonbiased assessment.

CHANGING SYSTEMS

Various changes have been attempted or proposed that effect broad and sweeping changes in the ways educators assess minority group children. For example, a moratorium on testing was advocated by the National Education Association (Bosma, 1973) and other groups, presumably to secure more equitable assessment techniques. However, a moratorium is a radical response that does not correct the problem. In fact, the contrary is being proposed: a basic tenet of nonbiased assessment is to require more testing, not less.

Offering cultural awareness seminars for the school staff also was used to facilitate work with minority group children and their families. The early seminars often were poorly planned. They raised expectations of significant changes in attitudes in a very short time. Yet the need for educators and psychologists to understand and be active in the minority communities remains a pressing need.

Screening and referral policies more recently have been examined as a source of bias (Ysseldyke, 1979). While there is a strong tendency to blame tests for putting children into ineffective programs, placement actually starts when teachers observe undesirable differences and subsequently refer children for special services. Information on bias associated with screening and referral is just beginning to be obtained and evaluated.

Many school systems have set informal quotas on the number of children from each racial or ethnic group included in their EMR programs and lower abilities groups. This is a political decision. It does not consider the real needs of children.

As was previously discussed, one way to effect changes toward nonbiased assessment has been by challenging school practices in the state and federal court systems (Bateman & Herr, in press; Laosa & Oakland, 1974; Ysseldyke & Shinn, in press). Typically a local school district or state education agency is made to defend its policies and practices by plaintiffs who initiate class action suits on behalf of a group of minority children. The resolution of allegations may occur by the plaintiffs and defendants negotiating with one another, by the court issuing a judgment of policies and procedures on nonbiased assessment, or by a court-appointed group of qualified experts who arrive at a decision.

State and federal legislation has provided strong influence regarding what constitutes basic nonbiased assessment programs. Of course, legislation carries with it the weight of the executive branch of government, which can force a school system to comply with the law. Clearly the most rapid progress toward defining appropriate nonbiased assessment practices has occurred through legislative and judicial actions.

CHANGING CHILDREN

Educators have attempted to improve assessment for minority group children by trying to improve their test-taking abilities and to encourage them to be more reflective and less impulsive in taking tests. This would allow them to more effectively express what they can and cannot do.

CONCLUSION

Significant advances have been made toward developing more appropriate assessment services with minority group children. Educators have a better understanding of the broad as well as specific problems, and they can anticipate and thus make provisions for potentially bias-producing points before, during, and

after assessment. Guidelines have been provided on which to base nonbiased programs.

However, educators are not ready to turn their attention elsewhere. Problems still exist. Educators need to discover better ways to help uncover and identify various talents and abilities that otherwise remain hidden and undeveloped. Better methods are needed of finding academic, cognitive, social, and emotional strengths which too often remain shrouded by bigotry, biases, poverty, or culture.

However, educators' responsibilities do not end by discovering talent. It is necessary to help foster the development of various abilities and talents. Once discovered, this information must be used to improve the development and status of all persons—to use test results to benefit children rather than to restrict their development or rigidify their status. Finally, educators are expected to help individuals make appropriate decisions. Children, parents, teachers, administrators, school board members, lawyers, judges, and others need reliable and valid information that is objectively obtained and offered.

Instead of using tests to limit educational and vocational opportunities, educators need to continue to seek ways to discover and foster talents. Instead of using tests to denigrate the dignity and pride of minority groups, educators must seek ways to destroy prejudicial attitudes and practices. Information should be used to set minds free and to humanize interpersonal relationships. Assessment techniques were developed to be of service to all citizens. Educators need to work to establish this principle in practice.

46 REFERENCES

American Psychological Association. *Ethical standards of psychologists*. Washington, D.C.: APA, 1972.

Bateman, B., & Herr, C. Law and special education. In J. M. Kauffman & D. P. Hallahan (Eds.), *Handbook of special education*. Englewood Cliffs, N.J.: Prentice-Hall, in press.

Bosma, B. The NEA testing moratorium. *Journal of School Psychology*, 1973, *11*, 304-306.

Cole, M., & Bruner, J. S. Cultural differences and inferences about psychological processes. *American Psychologist*, 1971, *26*, 867-876.

Cromwell, R. L., Blashfield, R. K., & Strauss, J. S. Criteria for classification systems. In N. Hobbs (Ed.), *Issues in the classification of children* (Vol. 1). San Francisco: Jossey-Bass, 1975.

Cronbach, L. J. Five decades of public controversy over mental testing. *American Psychologist*, 1975, *30*, 1-14.

Davis, F. *Standards for educational and psychological tests*. Washington, D.C.: American Psychological Association, 1974.

Drew, C. Criterion-referenced and norm-referenced assessment of minority group children. *Journal of School Psychology*, 1973, *11*, 323-329.

Eells, K. *Intelligence and cultural differences*. Chicago: University of Chicago Press, 1951.

Gerry, M. H. Cultural myopia: The need for a corrective lens. *Journal of School Psychology*, 1973, *11*, 307-315.

Green, D. *Racial and ethnic bias in test construction*. Monterey, Calif.: California Test Bureau/McGraw-Hill, no date.

Holmen, M. G., & Docter, R. *Educational and psychological testing*. New York: Russell Sage Foundation, 1972.

Jensen, A. J. Another look at culture-fair testing. In J. Hellmuth (Ed.), *Disadvantaged child*, Vol. 3, New York: Brunner/Mazel, 1970.

Jensen, A. J. *Test bias and construct validity*. Paper presented at the Annual Convention of the American Psychological Association, Chicago, September 1975.

Jensen, A. J. *Bias in mental testing*. New York: Free Press, 1980.

Laosa, L. M., & Oakland, T. D. Social control in mental health: Psychological assessment and the schools. Paper presented at the 51st Annual Meeting of the American Orthopsychiatric Association, San Francisco, April 1974.

Mercer, J. R., & Lewis, J. F. *System of multi-cultural pluralistic assessment* (SOMPA). New York: Psychological Corporation, 1978.

Newland, T. E. Assumptions underlying psychological testing. *Journal of School Psychology*, 1973, *11*, 315-322.

Oakland, T. D. Effects of test-wiseness materials on standardized test performance of preschool disadvantaged children. *Journal of School Psychology*, 1972, *10*, 355-360.

Oakland, T. D. Assessing minority group children: Challenges for school psychologists. *Journal of School Psychology*, 1973, *11*, 294-303.

Oakland, T. D. Assessment, education, and minority-group children. *Academic Therapy*, 1974, *10*, 133-140.

Oakland, T. D. Predictive validity of readiness tests for middle and lower socioeconomic status Anglo, black, and Mexican American children. *Journal of Educational Psychology*, 1978, *70*, 574-582.

Oakland, T. D., & Feigenbaum, D. Multiple sources of test bias on the WISC-R and Bender-Gestalt. *Journal of Consulting and Clinical Psychology*, 1979, *47*, 968-974.

Oakland, T. D., & Feigenbaum, D. Assessment of test bias on the Adaptive Behavior Inventory for Children. *Journal of School Psychology*, 1980, *18* (4).

Oakland, T. D., & Matuszek, P. Using tests in nondiscriminatory assessment. In T. D. Oakland (Ed.), *Psychological and educational assessment of minority group children*. New York: Brunner/Mazel, 1977.

Samuda, R. S. *Psychological testing of American minorities: Issues and consequences*. New York: Dodd, Mead & Co., 1975.

Sattler, J. Racial experimenter effects. In K. S. Miller & R. M. Dreger (Eds.), *Comparative studies of blacks and whites in the United States*. New York: Seminar Press, 1973.

Williams, R. Danger: Testing and dehumanizing black children. *The School Psychologist*, 1971, *25*, 11-13.

Ysseldyke, J. Issues in psychoeducational assessment. In D. Reschly and G. Phye (Eds.), *School psychology: Perspectives and issues*. New York: Academic Press, 1979.

Ysseldyke, J., and Shinn, M. Psychoeducational diagnosis. In J. M. Kauffman and D. P. Hallahan (Eds.), *Handbook of special education*. Englewood Cliffs, N. J.: Prentice-Hall, in press.

Thinking About Thinking About It in That Way: Test Data and Instruction

D. Kim Reid
University of Texas
Dallas, Texas

Wayne P. Hresko
North Texas State University
Denton, Texas

THE MANDATES of PL 94-142 have been double-edged. While they have sought to improve current testing practices, they have also served to promote testing as the sacred cow of educational decision making. Both norm-referenced and criterion-referenced tests have proliferated. (We are using the term *test* to refer to the use of formal or informal instruments and not to any systematic data collection that occurs under predetermined conditions.) Developers of norm-referenced tests have given considerable attention to statistical issues, although few tests used in special education meet the standards set for them (Salvia & Ysseldyke, 1978). Criterion-referenced tests have been designed to directly and absolutely assess whether students have acquired specific knowledge. These occurrences have led to increased willingness to rely on the results of testing as the primary basis for both diagnosis and teaching.

0196-6960/80/0013-0047$2.00
© 1980 Aspen Systems Corporation

We do not take issue with the use of norm-referenced tests for the purposes for which they were intended: to compare children's performances and to make judgments about their past rates of learning. Neither do we argue with the use of criterion-referenced tests for exploring children's performances vis-a-vis specific curriculum objectives. However, we assert that testing should *not* become the basis for curriculum design. (For detailed accounts of some reasons behind such an argument see Salvia & Ysseldyke, 1978; Tyron, 1979). An extension of that objection—and this will constitute the thrust of the discussion presented here—is that tests inappropriately constitute the major data source for making assertions about what children know and do not know for the purpose of teaching.

IF AN ANSWER IS WRONG

It is not unusual to hear an educator declare that Mary does not know certain information because she did not answer a question or a series of questions on a test—often a norm-referenced or criterion-referenced test on which the child's performance was analyzed item by item. That kind of analysis assumes that individuals always have access to everything they know—under all or nearly all circumstances. Although no exhaustive review of research has been attempted, we will give examples from research in developmental psychology, developmental psycholinguistics, and education to question the validity of such an assumption. Knowledge is not immutable (Das, Kirby, & Jarman, 1975). For example,

Mary's knowing a fact may not be sufficient to ensure that she will be able to recall it when a question designed to elicit that fact is presented. The same potential problems would exist if Mary were asked to define a word, to use a word in a sentence, or to apply a rule.

Of course, some levels of knowledge are more susceptible to problems of demonstration than others. Knowledge of facts, terms, rules, and principles, for example, may be easier to measure with assurance than knowledge of procedures, translations, or applications. However, even measures of direct recall are potentially misleading because forgetting is often rapid and even information in long-term storage is altered by experiences that follow its acquisition (Loftus & Loftus, 1980). Furthermore, unless test items are measures of direct recall, they are themselves problems of application. Bloom, Hastings, and Madaus (1971, p. 120) defined application as requiring the recognition of the essential aspects of the problem; determining the rules, principles, and generalizations that are relevant; and then using those ideas to solve a problem that has not been previously encountered. Although there is undoubtedly some information that may have no application (e.g., a state capital or the color of a dress), most of the objectives of schooling (especially reading, writing, and arithmetic) have validity only if they can be applied. Whatever the child's knowledge or level of functioning at the time of testing, however, the child may or may not think of bringing those abilities into play. Children may not "think of thinking about it in that way" (Duck-

Most of the objectives of schooling (especially reading, writing, and arithmetic) have validity only when they can be applied.

worth, 1979, p. 304). Therefore the question for educators is: Under what circumstances can the child bring knowledge into play? Answers may well be more closely related to one or more of the following considerations than to abstract "knowledge of the fact."

The complications that "thinking about thinking about it in that way" have on the interpretation of test data for educational planning are not limited to young or handicapped children. Duckworth (1979) described intelligent, adult students who experimented with floating and sinking objects for seven sessions before one of them thought about thinking that floating depends on weight and volume. Walter (cited in Duckworth) noted the amazement of an adult student trained in mathematics when she realized that moving one point of a rubber band to different points on the same row of a geoboard did not change the area of a triangle she had formed. She was so excited about her discovery that she shared it with the rest of the group, who also held degrees in mathematics. It was only after considerable discussion that they realized she had rediscovered a fact all of them had "known" since elementary school, namely, that the area of a triangle is half the base times the height. By moving only the apex of the triangle to another peg on the same row, she had maintained the area. Kuhn (1979) reported a similar

phenomenon in her work with a variety of persons ranging from preadolescent to elderly. Although many were unable to solve the problems she gave them, strategies appropriate to a successful problem solution were within their capacity, but for some reason they failed to use them.

Knowing How to Know

It is likely that what is measured by tests is as much a function of children's knowing how to know (Brown, 1975, 1978; Flavell, 1970, 1971, 1977; Flavell, Beach, & Chinsky, 1966; Flavell & Wellman, 1976); that is, the way they approach the task, as it is an estimate of what they in fact know. In the field of learning disabilities, for example, there is a body of literature accumulating that is impressive in regard to the consistency of its findings: learning disabled children (a) tend to approach problems with strategies characteristic of younger, normally achieving children; and (b) this delay in the spontaneous application of strategies appears to be approximately 2 years (Hallahan, 1975; Hallahan, Gajar, Cohen, & Tarver, 1978; Hallahan, Kauffman, & Ball, 1973; Hallahan, Tarver, Kauffman, & Graybeal, 1978; Tarver, Hallahan, Cohen, & Kauffman, 1977; Tarver, Hallahan, Kauffman, & Ball, 1976; Torgesen, 1977).

Wong's (1979) study of story comprehension in learning disabled and normally achieving children is illustrative. She first determined empirically what idea units (Brown & Smiley, 1977) were most important to the theme of a story. That story was then read to small groups of children as they read along. For the children in the

50

questions condition (half of each group), questions related to the thematically important idea units were embedded in the text prior to the paragraph in which the answer was contained. After the story was read to the children, they were asked to recall as much of it as possible. The number of units recalled provided a score.

As expected, normally achieving children in the no-question condition significantly outscored the learning disabled children in the same condition. However, a significant interaction effect indicated that in the question condition the learning disabled performed as well as the normally achieving children. The performance of normally achieving children did not improve as a result of having the questions available. Wong's explanation is that the normally achieving children were already using appropriate strategies in the recall task, so the use of questions did not help them. The learning disabled children, in contrast, appeared not to use strategies as effective as those used by the normally achieving children. Hence they benefited from the presence of the questions. Wong posited that "because the learning disabled children [in the question condition] read to answer the given questions, they ceased to be what Torgesen (1977) terms the inactive learner who typically does not participate in his/her learning" (p. 46).

However, the question arises whether the learning disabled children were "inactive" in the sense that they were not strategizing or whether they were using inferior, inefficient, or immature strategies. Work by a variety of professionals suggests the latter is true. Hallahan and colleagues (see Hallahan, 1975; Hallahan et al., 1978; Tarver et al., 1977) have found, for example, that learning disabled children exhibit immature strategies in both memory and attention tasks. Kershner (1975) and Reid and her colleagues (see Reid, 1980; Reid & Knight-Arest, 1980; Reid, Knight-Arest, & Hresko, 1980) have found that children with reading problems tend to continue the use of perceptually dominated strategies well after their agemates have shifted to more efficient, more cognitively oriented approaches to learning.

Some describe this problem as a production deficiency (Hall, 1980; Hallahan & Kneedler, 1979). A production deficiency occurs when children fail to use a strategy they are capable of using (Brown, 1975). One critical aspect of a production deficiency is that the child is able to use the ability when instructed to do so. For example, Spache (1976) reported that learning disabled children who had mastered phonics skills did not use them spontaneously while reading. However, they could use them when teachers instructed them to do so.

An Invalid Assumption

Making judgments about what children know for the purpose of teaching is therefore a complex chore. If teachers were interested in assessing children's knowledge of certain content, would it be more appropriate to consider their knowledge that which they can recall with questions or without them? If teachers are interested in teaching them to read, perhaps the decision would be different. Do children who use phonic analysis only when specifically instructed to do so really "know" phonics? What is the validity of teaching a curriculum to mastery on test performance when the only real purpose for such instruction is to enable children to use those skills whenever they need them to assist in reading? Assuming that what children demonstrate they can do by taking a test reflects their knowledge clearly is not an adequate basis for instructional planning.

IF THE ANSWER IS RIGHT

The complementary issue in the interpretation of test data for instructional purposes is this: Can one be assured that a child who answers a question or set of questions correctly on a test does in fact know the material? The answer may be yes—or it may be that the child was able to succeed by guessing or by using information contained in the questions themselves to decipher an appropriate answer. De Villiers and de Villiers (1978, p. 99), for example, asked a child, "Is it upside-down, hm?" The child responded, "It upaside-down." That certainly appeared to be a correct response. But further questioning led to a different assessment of the child's competence. When the adult asked "What kind of truck is it, Billy?" the child answered, "It's a kind of truck." He had learned that something in the question had something to do with the answer he should give. The strategy he adopted was, at least in some instances, successful and gave the appearance that he had abilities that he had not in fact mastered. These are obvious problems of

which educators tend to be aware and which are minimal when well-constructed, individually administered tests are used.

Following are two other points important to consider if one is planning to teach a child: (a) that the child may have learned a verbal rule but does not really understand the concept behind it and (b) that giving a correct response does not tell the examiner whether a child can use that knowledge.

Verbal Rule Learning

Knight-Arest and Reid (1980) conducted a study in which learning disabled and normally achieving children were invited to a party in groups of three (always classmates together). One child—previously determined to be the only one of the three children who was a nonconserver—was asked to pour juice for his two friends. The nonconserver and one of the other children had short, wide glasses. The second conserver had a tall, thin glass. The children were instructed not to drink the juice until all had agreed that the pouring was fair. Of course, once the nonconserver poured the juice in the tall, thin glass only up to the level of the juice in the short, wide glasses, the conservers began arguing for a fairer apportionment. The investigator did not intervene, but only recorded the arguments the conservers used to convince the nonconserver that the child with the tall, thin glass deserved more juice. After the children agreed that the pouring was fair, the party was held. Within a day, a comparable conservation-of-liquids task was ad-

52

ministered to the children who had been nonconservers, and the reasons they gave to support their decisions were recorded.

Statistically there was no difference in the number of normally achieving or learning disabled children who could conserve on the posttest. However, there were striking differences in their reasons. The normally achieving children were able to give reasons for their conservation responses that were not offered by their peers during the party (a phenomenon that has also been documented by Doise & Perret-Clermont, 1975). Although the learning disabled children were also giving conservation responses, their reasons were limited to those they had heard from their peers. On a delayed posttest (2 weeks later), a very high percentage of the normally achieving children had maintained the conservation response. However, there were significantly fewer learning disabled children who continued to give conservation responses. It appears that the learning disabled children had acquired a verbal rule without understanding. They were able to give correct answers shortly after the learning experience, but once the advantage of recency was lost, the learning disabled children were no longer able to remember or apply the rule.

Another well-known example of the same problem is Engelmann's (1971) teaching conservation-of-volume responses using a verbal rule strategy to a group of young children. Engelmann was free to instruct the group of students until he was satisfied that they had reached criterion performance. At that point, Kamii and Derman (1971) reexamined the children, pressing them to explain their answers. They concluded that the children had learned only a rote application of the rule.

Because the children can give a rule, it appears that they have understood the rule. But in fact they may only have memorized it. They may be repeating empty words. Many times the right answer may be given on Monday, but the child fails the same item if he or she is retested a few days later. Perhaps memorizing without understanding accounts in some measure for learning disabled and retarded children's inability to retain what they have learned.

Functional Language

The study of pragmatics in developmental psycholinguistics raises similar questions about reliance on test data for instructional planning. Pragmatics refers to the functional use of language in interpersonal communication. Basic to using language is being able to ask questions when you need to know something: it is important to know what you do not know. Also important are understanding and responding to the other participants' needs in the interaction, and knowing how to say the "right thing in the right way at the right time and place. . . ." (Ervin-Tripp, 1971, p. 37).

Because the children can give a rule, it appears that they have understood the rule. But in fact they may only have memorized it.

Passing test items measuring vocabulary, sentence repetition, inflectional endings, and the like does not ensure that children are effective language users. Bloom and Lahey (1978, p. 290) noted that children with language disorders or disabilities "may have learned something about the world and something about the conventional code, but are unable to *use* the code in speaking or understanding in certain contexts or for certain purposes." They indicate that the effect of language impairment in some children is that they do not verbalize. Yet when these same children are prodded into verbalization during testing, they do well. They have the code, but do not understand its use. This impairment in the ability to *use* language is noted in the literature related to the mentally retarded and the emotionally disturbed (Bloom & Lahey, 1978).

In research with learning disabled children, *use* problems have been identified by a number of independent investigators. Use problems have been related to fillers (Wiig & Semel, 1976), lack of verbal fluency (Bryan, 1974), overuse of a limited, concrete vocabulary (Wiig & Semel, 1976), use of pronouns without antecedents (Reid & Knight-Arest, 1980), and giving misinformation or failing to clarify correct information (Bryan & Pflaum, 1978). However, prior testing had revealed that the children were capable of defining vocabulary words and had knowledge of pronouns. Performance in a game requiring give and take of information with hyperactive children indicated less efficient language use with respect to answering and asking questions and giving and using feedback (Whalen, Henker,

Collins, McAuliffe, & Vaux, 1979). Knowing something about vocabulary or syntax does not guarantee competent language use. Most tests of language used with exceptional children do not include any measure of *how* children use their language knowledge. Muma (1978) suggested that in a test setting, examination of language usage probably cannot be accomplished.

In summary, if a child's answer on a test is correct, that does not necessarily mean that the child knows the correct answer. It means that he or she knows under those circumstances. Similarly, children who succeed on test items often fail to use that knowledge in the day-to-day situations in which its use would be appropriate. If educators are comparing children's standing with that of their peers or are screening them for curriculum placements, testing (norm-referenced and criterion-referenced) makes good sense. But if the aim is to teach children, teachers cannot take for granted that children know what the tests indicate they know.

DEPTH OF KNOWLEDGE

There is one additional consideration to note in regard to the interpretation of test answers. It is often important to teachers to know *how* an answer was formulated. Examples will be taken from the research on analogical reasoning and metaphorical language, since they are both curriculum objectives and familiar question types.

A number of researchers have shown that young children can both understand and produce metaphors (Billow, 1975) but require the complex reasoning abilities

54

not developed until adolescence to appreciate the figurative meaning (Gallagher & Wright, 1977; Ortony, 1979). Hillman's (1980) research with adolescents' analogical reasoning highlighted this distinction. She argued that answers to analogy problems reflect experiences children have with the content of the analogies, general intelligence, and facility with language. If the purpose of testing is comparison to a normative group, those factors do not necessarily hinder interpretation of the child's performance. However, if the purpose of testing is to plan to teach children analogies or metaphorical language, one would need to know *why* the response was given. Hillman reported that one of the adolescents she tested gave the response mare to the analogy Horse is to _______ as cow is to calf (p. 94). Asked to explain her answer, the child replied, "Because a mare is a baby horse as a calf is a baby cow" (p. 64). The response was incorrect, because the child was not familiar with the vocabulary—not because the child did not understand the structure of analogies. (Of course, it was recognition of such problems that led Piaget to conduct his early research.) This difference would not be important in norm-referenced testing, but it would be important to make such a distinction if criterion-referenced tests were being used. Although their major function is to provide data relevant to instruction, few criterion-referenced tests are designed to reveal the nature of the error.

CONCLUSIONS

It is frequently argued that valid and reliable norm-referenced tests provide teachers with considerable information useful to teaching. Writing of this article was motivated by recent experiences in four states in two separate sections of the country in which teachers, school psychologists, and educational diagnosticians relied heavily on the results of standardized testing for both diagnostic evaluations and the development of individualized education programs (IEPs). Some of the professionals with whom we worked acknowledged that tests measuring pervasive cognitive and psychomotor abilities contribute relatively little to the development of the IEP once a diagnosis has been made.

However, nearly all of them maintained that achievement tests—either norm-referenced or criterion-referenced—that provide information about a child's performance on particular items or objectives were useful in IEP development. Most of these individuals were firmly convinced that children's performance on a criterion-referenced test characterized the state of their knowledge. Educational planning was based on the accomplishment of objectives derived from testing. Long-range goals were set for a full year and short-term objectives devised for several months. Often the periodic review of the IEP and its revisions was based on additional testing, especially criterion-referenced tests.

There is no difficulty in this approach if school professionals recognize test performances as samples of behavior that do not necessarily reflect a child's state of knowledge. Lawler (cited in Zivian, 1977) noted that test items that most children pass (or fail) are not included in standardized tests. Test scores may therefore obscure what children know. But tests and test scores tend to be both seductive and viewed as accurate. When the results of instruction do not match anticipated outcomes, instead of considering that a child may have performed well on a test or poorly on a test for reasons such as those presented above, school personnel tend to be surprised that the child learned so easily or forgot so rapidly.

Even more important, reliance on tests as indicators of children's progress diverts attention from the only true evaluation that can be accomplished: ongoing daily appraisal. Many teachers who use test data regularly do not keep careful records of children's responses to questions or ap-

---

Reliance on tests as indicators of children's progress diverts attention from the only true evaluation that can be accomplished: ongoing appraisal day by day.

---

proaches to learning. Instead tests are given at the end of units or lessons—after the child has already succeeded or failed—and children are either advanced to new objectives or are left to repeat the old ones.

We agree with Wallace and Larsen (1978) that testing for teaching must be continuous. But we would go one step beyond their recommendations by suggesting that it is also necessary to test the test results. Only through continuing dialogue with students and continued observation, probing, and record keeping can teachers determine what strategies children use to approach tasks, whether they have learned only to verbalize a rule or whether they really understand, whether they can *use* the information they have learned, and what depth of understanding they have attained. Knowledge of all of these outcomes is necessary for educational planning, but test data do not provide these observations.

REFERENCES

Billow, R. M. A cognitive developmental study of metaphor comprehension. *Developmental Psychology*, 1975, *11*, 415-423.

Bloom, B. S., Hastings, J. T., & Madaus, G. S. *Handbook on formative and summative evaluation of student learning.* New York: McGraw-Hill, 1971.

Bloom, L., & Lahey, L. *Language development and language disorders.* New York: John Wiley & Sons, 1978.

Brown, A. L. The development of memory: Knowing, knowing about knowing, knowing how to know. In H. W. Reese (Ed.), *Advances in child development and behavior (Vol. 10).* New York: Academic Press, 1975.

Brown, A. L. Knowing when, where, and how to remember: A problem of metacognition. In R. Glaser (Ed.), *Advances in instructional psychology.* Hillsdale, N.J.: Lawrence Erlbaum Associates, 1978.

Brown, A. L., & Smiley, S. S. Rating the importance of structural units of prose passages: A problem of metacognitive development. *Child Development*, 1977, *48*, 1-8.

Bryan, T. Peer popularity of learning-disabled children. *Journal of Learning Disabilities*, 1974, *7*, 261-268.

Bryan, T., & Pflaum, S. Social interactions of learning disabled children: A linguistic, social, and cognitive analysis. *Learning Disabilities Quarterly*, 1978, *1*, 70-79.

Das, J. P., Kirby, J., & Jarman, R. F. Simultaneous and successive syntheses: An alternative model for cognitive abilities. *Psychological Bulletin*, 1975, *82*, 87-103.

de Villiers, J. G., & de Villiers, P. A. *Language acquisition.* Cambridge, Mass.: Harvard University Press, 1978.

56

Doise, W., & Perret-Clermont, A. W. Social interaction and the development of cognitive operations. *European Journal of Social Psychology*, 1975, *5*, 367-383.

Duckworth, E. Either we're too early and they can't learn it or we're too late and they know it already: The dilemma of "Applying Piaget." *Harvard Educational Review*, 1979, *49*, 297-312.

Engelmann, S. E. Does the Piagetian approach imply instruction? In D. R. Green, M. P. Ford, & G. P. Flamer (Eds.), *Measurement and Piaget*. New York: McGraw-Hill, 1971.

Ervin-Tripp, S. Social backgrounds and verbal skills. In R. Huxley & E. Ingram (Eds.), *Language acquisition: Models and methods*. New York: Academic Press, 1971.

Flavell, J. H. Developmental studies of mediated memory. In H. W. Reese & L. P. Lipsitt (Eds.), *Advances in child development and behavior, Vol. 5*. New York: Academic Press, 1970.

Flavell, J. H. First discussant's comments: What is memory development the development of? *Human Development*, 1971, *14*, 272-278.

Flavell, J. H. *Cognitive development*. Englewood Cliffs, N.J.: Prentice-Hall, 1977.

Flavell, J. H., Beach, D. H., & Chinsky, J. M. Spontaneous verbal rehearsal in a memory task as a function of age. *Child Development*, 1966, *37*, 283-299.

Flavell, J. H., & Wellman, H. M. Metamemory. In R. V. Kail & J. W. Hagen (Eds.), *Memory in cognitive development*. Hillsdale, N.J.: Lawrence Erlbaum Associates, 1976.

Gallagher, J. M., & Wright, R. J. Children's solution of verbal analogies: Extension of Piaget's concept of reflexive abstraction. Paper presented in the symposium "Thinking with the left hand: Children's understanding of analogy and metaphor." Society for Research in Child Development, New Orleans, 1977.

Hall, R. J. Cognitive behavior modification and information processing skills of exceptional children. *Exceptional Education Quarterly*, 1980, *1*(1), 9-15.

Hallahan, D. P. Distractibility in the learning disabled child. In W. M. Cruickshank & D. P. Hallahan (Eds.), *Perceptual and learning disabilities in children, Vol. 2: Research and theory*. Syracuse, N.Y.: Syracuse University Press, 1975.

Hallahan, D. P., Gajar, A. H., Cohen, S. B., & Tarver, S. G. Selective attention and locus of control in learning disabled and normal children. *Journal of Learning Disabilities*, 1978, *11*, 231-236.

Hallahan, D. P., Kauffman, J. M., & Ball, D. W. Selective attention and cognitive tempo of low achieving and high achieving sixth grade males. *Perceptual and Motor Skills*, 1973, *36*, 579-583.

Hallahan, D. P., & Kneedler, R. D. Strategy deficits in the information processing of learning disabled children. Technical Report No. 6, University of Virginia Learning Disabilities Research Institute, Charlottesville, 1979.

Hallahan, D. P., Tarver, S. G., Kauffman, J. M., & Graybeal, N. L. A comparison of the effects of reinforcement and response cost on the selective attention of learning disabled children. *Journal of Learning Disabilities*, 1978, *11*, 430-438.

Hillman, I. D. A developmental study of sex, aspiration and the onset of formal operations. Unpublished doctoral dissertation, New York University, 1980.

Kamii, C., & Derman, L. Comments on Engelmann's paper. In D. R. Greene, M. P. Ford, & G. P. Flamer (Eds.), *Measurement and Piaget*. New York: McGraw-Hill, 1971.

Kershner, J. R. Visual-spatial organization and reading: Support for a cognitive developmental interpretation. *Journal of Learning Disabilities*, 1975, *8*, 30-36.

Knight-Arest, I., & Reid, D. K. Peer interaction as a catalyst for conservation acquisition in normal and learning disabled children. *Proceedings of the Ninth Interdisciplinary International Conference on Piagetian Theory and the Helping Professions*, Los Angeles, 1980.

Kuhn, D. The application of Piaget's theory of cognitive development to education. *Harvard Educational Review*, 1979, *49*, 340-360.

Loftus, E. S., & Loftus, G. R. On the permanence of stored information in the human brain. *American Psychologist*, 1980, *35*, 409-420.

Muma, J. R. *Language handbook: Concepts, assessment, intervention*. Englewood Cliffs, N.J.: Prentice-Hall, 1978.

Ortony, A. Beyond literal similarity. *Psychological Review*, 1979, *86*, 161-182.

Reid, D. K. Learning from a Piagetian perspective: The exceptional child. In I. E. Sigel, R. M. Golinkoff, & D. Brodzinsky (Eds.), *Piagetian theory and research: New directions and applications*. Hillsdale, N.J.: Lawrence Erlbaum Associates, 1980.

Reid, D. K., & Knight-Arest, I. Cognitive processing in normally achieving and learning disabled boys. In M. Freidman (Ed.), *Intelligence and learning*. New York: Plenum, 1980.

Reid, D. K., Knight-Arest, I., & Hresko, W. P. The development of cognition in learning disabled children. In J. Gottlieb & S. S. Strichart (Eds.), *Developmental theories and research in learning disabilities*. Baltimore: University Park Press, 1980.

Salvia, J., & Ysseldyke, J. E. *Assessment in special and remedial education*. Dallas: Houghton Mifflin Co., 1978.

Spache, G. D. *Diagnosing and correcting reading disabilities*. Boston: Allyn and Bacon, 1976.

Tarver, S. G., Hallahan, D. P., Cohen, S. B., & Kauffman, J. M. The development of visual selective attention and verbal rehearsal on learning disabled boys. *Journal of Learning Disabilities*, 1977, *10*, 491-500.

Tarver, S. G., Hallahan, D. P., Kauffman, J. M., & Ball, D. W. Verbal rehearsal and selective attention in children with learning disabilities: A developmental lag. *Journal of Experimental Child Psychology*, 1976, *22*, 375-385.

Torgesen, J. K. The role of nonspecific factors in the task performance of learning disabled children: A theoretical assessment. *Journal of Learning Disabilities*, 1977, *10*, 27-34.

Torgesen, J. K., & Goldman, T. Verbal rehearsal and short-term memory in reading-disabled children. *Child Development*, 1977, *48*, 56-60.

Torgesen, J. K., Murphy, H. A., & Ivey, C. The influence of an orienting task on the memory performance of children with reading problems. *Journal of Learning Disabilities*, 1979, *12*, 396-401.

Tyron, W. W. The test-trait fallacy. *American Psychologist*, 1979, *34*, 402-406.

Wallace, G., & Larsen, S. C. *Educational assessment of learning problems: Testing for teaching*. Boston: Allyn and Bacon, 1978.

Whalen, C. K., Henker, B., Collins, B. E., McAuliffe, S., & Vaux, A. Peer interaction in a structured communication task: Comparisons of normal and hyperactive boys and of methylphenidate (Ritalin) and placebo effects. *Child Development*, 1979, *50*, 388-401.

Wiig, E. H., & Semel, E. M. *Language disabilities in children and adolescents*. Columbus, Ohio: Charles E. Merrill, 1976.

Wong, B. Y. L. Increasing retention of main ideas through questioning strategies. *Learning Disabilities Quarterly*, 1979, *2*, 42-47.

Zivian, N. T. Dialectics: Paradigms for the social sciences. *Human Development*, 1977, *20*, 249-252.

Measurement of Functional Competencies and the Handicapped: Constructs, Assessments, and Recommendations

J. Lee Wiederholt
Mary E. Cronin
University of Texas
Austin, Texas

Virginia Stubbs
Texas Association for Children
with Learning Disabilities
Austin, Texas

IN RECENT YEARS, parents· and professionals have voiced growing concern over the competencies of youngsters. As a result a majority of states have recently initiated and passed legislation mandating assessment of the functional competencies of high school students. This article addresses the assessment of competencies in regard to the handicapped student (see also, article by Pullin, EEQ 1:2). The first part discusses the construct of functional competencies. The second part contains an overview of current assessment practices. The final part makes recommendations on the handicapped and the measurement of their competencies.

THE CONSTRUCT OF FUNCTIONAL COMPETENCY

Kerlinger (1979) defines a *construct* as a concept with a specified meaning given to it by individuals. To adequately address

0196-6960/80/0013-0059$2.00

60

the topic of functional competencies, it is essential that the term be understood. Therefore this part presents a brief overview of the historical development of the concept of functional competency and the terminology associated with this construct.

History

Functional competency was first referred to as "literacy." Before the 1870s a literate person was one who could leave one's "mark" (signature) on stone, wood, or paper. During the 1870s and 1880s the ability to read a simple passage as well as the ability to write one's name became the indicator of a literate person. By 1890, society required additional writing of a literate person, such as personal correspondence and record keeping (Grattan, 1959).

World War I recruits were considered literate by the federal government if they could read, write, and comprehend a 2,800-word vocabulary. In addition, a reading speed of 150 words per minute was also necessary to demonstrate literacy (Cook, 1977).

After World War II the United Nations Education, Scientific, and Cultural Organization (UNESCO) developed a definition of literacy to be used worldwide. The official UNESCO definition stated that literacy was the ability to read and write a short simple statement of everyday life with understanding. In 1965 the U.S. Office of Education (USOE) established a national norm for literacy. The USOE norm coupled satisfactory achievement of four years of elementary school with the ability to function in society. Functional literacy included math, reading, and writing ability as well as a general understanding of everyday life—for example, banking, working, maintaining a home.

As can be seen, the historical progression of the construct of functional competency has moved from the most rudimentary form of signing one's name to a more complex concept. Today functional competency appears to be viewed by large governmental agencies as the ability to live independently, through use of skills in reading, writing, and math.

Terminology

The term *functional competency* in this article describes the construct of basic skills or independent living. Schools sometimes add the word *minimal* to this term. The term *minimal functional competencies* appears to refer to those skills that are presumed to be the most basic within the construct. While the latter term is most associated with this construct in schools today, other terms have frequently been used to describe basic skills or independent living. Table 1 lists related terms, the person(s) suggesting them, and their definitions.

An analysis of the terms reveals relationships in their specific areas of focus,

---

The historical progression of the construct of functional competencies has moved from the most rudimentary form of signing one's name to a much more complex concept.

Table 1
Terminology Related to Functional Competency

Terminology	Author/Date	Definition
Literacy	Bormuth, 1975	Ability to respond competently to real world tasks.
	Davis, 1977	The level of one's functioning in any skill area that is generally considered necessary in today's society.
	Dauzat & Dauzat, 1977	Defined by its properties: (a) economic value, (b) personal-social value, and (c) political value.
	Elgin, 1978	Ability to read with sufficient pleasure and write with sufficient ease so that both activities become a part of one's daily life that one would be unwilling to give up.
	Wiemann, 1978	Reading, writing, speaking, and listening.
Basic literacy	Powell, 1977	Ability to use correspondence of visual shapes to spoken words in order to decode written material and translate into oral language.
Functional literacy	Miller, 1973	Ability to read (decode and comprehend) materials needed to perform everyday vocational tasks.
	Buchanan, 1975	Rudimentary social literacy—that is, those skills required by a prospective employer or institution that a student is deemed likely to encounter in adult life.
	Sticht, 1975	Possession of those skills needed to successfully perform some reading task imposed by an external agent between reader and a goal the reader wishes to obtain based on demand of reading task, not skill level.
Civilized literacy	Buchanan, 1975	Skills and knowledge derived from reading that provide guides to the exercise of power, reason, and virtue.
Survival skills	Norton, 1979	Competence needed for personal growth for successful existence as citizens, consumers, job holders, taxpayers, and members of families.
Basic skills	Lieb-Brilhart, 1977	Areas of listening, speaking, reading, writing, and arithmetic represent areas fundamental to literacy.
Competence	Murphy, 1975	Reading skills suitable for adequate functioning in normal day-to-day life.
Communicative competence	Larson, 1978	Ability to demonstrate a knowledge of the socially appropriate communicative behaviors in a given situation.
Functional illiteracy	Cook, 1977	Cannot read or write to survive everyday tasks.
	Smith, 1977	Cannot function effectively in their particular occupation, their community, or society.
Illiteracy	Harman, 1970	Inability to read and write a simple message either in English or any other language.

62

which cluster around the following five areas:

1. *Vocational or job related competency:* Buchanan (1975), Miller (1973), and Smith (1977);
2. *Daily adult life:* Bormuth (1975), Cook (1977), Davis (1977), Elgin (1978), Larson (1978), Murphy (1975) and Norton (1979);
3. *Skills in reading, writing, speaking, listening, and math:* Harman (1970), Lieb-Brilhart (1977), Powell (1977), Sticht (1975), and Wiemann (1978);
4. *Philosophical competency:* Buchanan (1975); and
5. *Ability to attain goals:* Dauzat and Dauzat (1977).

Authors also may use the same term but define it somewhat differently. For example, both Bormuth (1975) and Davis (1977) use the term *literacy,* but Bormuth defines it as the ability to respond competently to real-world tasks. Davis, in contrast, defines it as the level of one's functioning in any skill area that is generally considered necessary in today's society. Both definitions are obviously related or have a similar focus. However, when one compares the definitions of *functional literacy,* one can note some obvious differences in focus. For example, Sticht (1975) limits functional literacy to reading, while Buchanan (1975) focuses on social behaviors.

Other authorities avoided using only one term when defining the construct of functional competency and instead focused on graduated levels of the concept. In other words, they might distinguish between preliteracy and functional literacy. The graduated levels and definitions

for each level suggested by four writers are shown in Table 2.

Robinson (1963) outlined what he called a "stairway of [reading] literacy" consisting of five levels. These levels ranged from complete illiteracy (unable to read English at all) to complete literacy (ability to read effectively, adjusting rate and approach to purpose and difficulty of material). Miller (1973) divided literacy into three categories: basic literacy, comprehension literacy, and functional or practical literacy. He postulated that decoding and comprehension are necessary before a person can read the materials required to perform everyday vocational tasks.

The adult performance level (APL) (Northcutt, 1975) divided functional competency into three levels, of which income, education, and job status were the criteria. The lower a person's income, education, and job status, the lower his or her performance level. The APL project outlined four aspects of a general theory instead of a definition of adult functional competency.

First, functional competency was seen as a construct that is meaningful only in a specific societal context. For example, the person who is functionally competent in one society may be incompetent in another. Also, as the technology of the society changes, the requirements for competency change. Second, functional competency was seen as two-dimensional and was described as the application of a set of skills (reading, writing, etc.) to a set of general knowledge areas (occupational knowledge, health, etc.). Third, a person was viewed as functionally competent

Table 2
Levels of Functional Competencies

Terms	Author/Date	Definition
1. Complete illiteracy	Robinson, 1963	1. Unable to read English at all.
2. Low-level literacy		2. Able to read at grade levels 1-4. Barely able to contend with the adult reading material available.
3. Partial literacy		3. Able to read at grade levels 5-6. Just able to read essential information for daily living and working at low levels.
4. Variable literacy		4. Able to read many kinds of materials at a variety of levels.
5. Complete literacy		5. Able to read effectively, suiting reading rate and approach to purposes and difficulty of material.
1. Basic literacy	Miller, 1973	1. Ability to use correspondences of visual shapes to spoken sounds in order to decode written materials and translate into oral language.
2. Comprehension literacy		2. Ability to understand the meaning of verbal materials.
3. Functional or practical literacy		3. Ability to read (decode and comprehend) materials needed to perform everyday vocational needs.
Level 1	Northcutt, 1975	1. Adults who function with difficulty (income poverty level or less, 8 years of school or fewer, and unemployment or low-status jobs).
Level 2		2. Functional adults (income above poverty level but no discretionary income, education of 9 to 11 years of school, and menial-job-status occupations).
Level 3		3. Proficient adults (high levels of income, 12 years of school or more, and high levels of job status).
Preliteracy level Basic literacy level Functional or career literacy level	Powell, 1977	Sees literacy as the universe and the general indicator levels as subsystems in an ongoing process with each level developing out of previous levels.

64

only to the extent that he or she could meet the requirements extant at a given time. Functional competency was seen as a dynamic rather than a static state. Fourth, functional competency was viewed as directly related to success in adult life. More competent adults were expected to be more successful.

Finally, Powell (1977) saw literacy as the universe and the general indicator levels as subsystems. He suggested three subsets designated as the preliteracy level, the basic literacy level, and the functional (practical) or career literacy level. At the preliteracy level the person is just beginning to obtain knowledge and use of language as well as the computational processes essential for literacy. Skills are considered unstable at this level. At the basic literacy level the skills are believed to become permanent, automatic, and generative. They can be used on demand and develop without formal instruction. The career literacy level that Powell suggested was not as stable nor as generative as the previous level but depended on the knowledge base of the preliteracy and basic literacy levels. Powell believed that because demands and tasks vary with every occupation, specialized requirements and the level of knowledge and skill would also vary accordingly.

The apparent lack of agreement regarding the construct of functional competency is probably directly related to the lack of research. Few reliable data concerning what makes one group of people competent and another group incompetent are available. Because the construct is often defined in an encompassing and general manner (i.e., the ability to function independently in life), a person undoubtedly requires several skills and abilities before he or she can achieve this independence. Until empirical data are available, it is likely that the construct of functional competency will continue to be ill defined and incompletely understood.

Despite the lack of agreement among scholars about what functional competency is, many school personnel are now legally required to assess their students' skills and abilities in this area. This is a difficult task because a universally accepted definition of the construct is not available. How professionals in the nation's schools approach this task is the problem discussed next.

CURRENT ASSESSMENT PRACTICES

Although the construct is defined in many different ways, most states require that their students be tested for functional competency. Pipho (1979) recently compiled an extensive list of state activities regarding competency testing. The data the authors found most relevant to the topic of this article (the areas to be tested by the 38 states that require competency testing,) are shown in Table 3.

Until empirical data are available, it is likely that the construct of functional competencies will continue to be ill defined and incompletely understood.

Some states indicate assessment of general skill areas (basic skills, life skills, basic communication skills, etc.). Others measure specific skills areas (reading, writing, and math) as an indicator of a functionally competent person. Reading is the testing area with the highest percentage (74%) followed by math (68%) and writing (45%). Some skill areas probably overlap—for example, reading and reading comprehension, as well as math and computation, as used in California. The meaning of the specific differentiation between mathematics and computation or the distinctions among any other overlapping skill areas are unclear, partly because the tests are difficult to obtain for inspection. Elgin (1978, p. 10) has stated this problem well:

> You may not have had the opportunity to examine the literacy tests lately. They are not easy to look at. Even someone like myself, armed with all the required academic credentials and legitimately funded for research on the question, requires something approaching an Act of Congress to obtain access to them.

Obviously, one reason the tests are difficult to obtain is the fear that if they are made widely available, then the tests will be taught to students. However, the authors cannot help wondering about the rationale for selection of items and tests, the standardization data on these measures, and the reliability and validity of the results.

Table 3 provides an overall picture of the variability in competency testing throughout the United States for non-handicapped students. Another survey was recently completed by the National Association of State Directors of Special Education (NASDSE). This survey determined the extent of competency testing and the awarding of diplomas for the handicapped population (Linde, 1979). Table 4 provides a summary of some of the data in the NASDSE survey. Of the 54 states and territories surveyed, 17 have established some form of competency testing for the handicapped. Two of these states, Tennessee and Hawaii, will require competency testing in 1982 and 1983, respectively. Idaho leaves the decision regarding testing to the local school boards.

Six states require handicapped students to take the competency tests. Florida requires that only the speech and language impaired, visually impaired, and orthopedically impaired be tested. Massachussetts designates evaluation teams to decide on an individual basis whether handicapped students should be included in the testing program. New York requires all but the retarded to participate in competency testing. California, Maryland, and Vermont require that all handicapped students take the competency tests.

A total of seven states are either providing or are in the process of developing special testing procedures for the handicapped population. California, Florida, Nebraska, and New York are implementing special procedures for administering competency tests to the handicapped population. Hawaii, Massachusetts, and Vermont are currently studying or developing special testing procedures for handicapped students.

Table 3
Skill Areas Assessed by States*

Columns CED, APL and To be determined are grouped under the heading "Other options."

State	Setting of standards†	Reading	Reading comprehension	Application of reading	Mathematics	Computation	Consumer economics	Government/economics	Language arts	Grammar	Spelling	Writing	Application of writing	Composition	Basic communication skills	Listening skills	Speaking skills	Career development	Personal development	Cultural arts	Basic skill areas	Functional literacy	Life skills	Survival skills	Local district option	CED	APL	To be determined
Alabama	SDE	●			●							●																
Arizona	Both	●				●						●																
Arkansas	SBE	●			●																							
California	Both	●	●		●	●	●					●																
Colorado	LB																								●			
Connecticut	Both	●			●				●																	●	●	
Delaware	SDE			●	●								●															
Florida	Both																				●	●						
Georgia	SDE/SBE	●			●													●										
Idaho	SBE	●			●						●	●																
Illinois	Both																								●			
Indiana	LB	●									●																	
Kansas	SDE/SBE	●			●									●									●					
Kentucky	SDE	●			●				●		●	●																
Louisiana	SSS					●									●													
Maine	SDE	●			●							●																
Maryland	SBE	●																										
Massachusetts	LB				●										●	●	●											
Michigan	SDE	●			●																							
Missouri	SDE			●	●			●																				
Nebraska	LB	●			●							●																
Nevada	SBE	●			●							●																
New Hampshire	SDE				●										●													
New Jersey	SDE/SBE	●			●							●											●					

Table 3 (Continued)
Skill Areas Assessed by States*

State	Setting of standards†	Reading	Reading comprehension	Application of reading	Mathematics	Computation	Consumer economics	Government/economics	Language arts	Grammar	Spelling	Writing	Application of writing	Composition	Basic communication skills	Listening skills	Speaking skills	Career development	Personal development	Cultural arts	Basic skill areas	Functional literacy	Life skills	Survival skills	Local district option (Other options)	CED (Other options)	APL (Other options)	To be determined (Other options)
New Mexico	SDE											●																●
New York	SBR	●			●							●																
North Carolina	●●																											●
Oklahoma	None	●																						●				
Oregon	LB	●				●						●						●	●									
Rhode Island	SSC/SBR	●			●				●											●			●					
South Carolina	SBE	●			●							●																
Tennessee	Both	●			●					●	●																	
Texas	State	●			●				●			●																
Utah	LB	●			●		●	●				●				●	●											
Vermont	SBE	●			●							●				●	●											
Virginia	Both	●			●										●								●					
Washington	LB	●			●				●																			
Wyoming	LB	●				●		●				●																
No. of states		28	1	2	26	5	2	3	5	1	4	17	1	1	4	3	3	2	1	1	1	1	4	1	2	1	2	1
Percentage of states (of 38)		74	3	5	68	13	5	8	13	3	11	45	3	3	11	8	8	5	3	3	3	3	11	3	5	3	5	3

*Data compiled from information presented by Chris Pipho, Education Commission of the States, July 1979 (grant no. NIE-G-79-0033).

†LB, Local board decision; SBE, state board of education decision; SDE, state department of education decision; Both, state and local decision; SSS, state superintendent of schools; ●●, Competency test commission; SSC, state standards council; SBR, state board of regents.

Table 4
Summary of NASDSE Survey*
on Competency Testing of Handicapped Children

State	Mandatory competency test for graduation	Handicaps required for student to take test									Special procedures	Regular diplomas	Special diplomas	Certificate of attendance
		EMR	TMR	LD	SP/Lang	ED	VI	HI	OI	MH				
Alabama	No											Yes		
Alaska	No											LB		No
Am. Samoa	No											Yes		No
Arizona	No											LB	LB	No
Arkansas	No											LB		
California	Yes	•	•	•	•	•	•	•	•	•	Yes	LB		LB
Colorado	No											LB		LB
Connecticut	Yes											LB	LB	LB
Delaware	Yes											Yes		No
Dist. Col.	No											Yes		Yes
Florida	Yes				•		•		•		Yes	Yes	Yes	Yes
Georgia	No											LB	LB	LB
Guam	No											Yes		No
Hawaii	Yes 1983										Yes 1983	Yes		Yes
Idaho	LB											Yes		No
Illinois	No											Yes		
Indiana	No											Yes		LB
Iowa	No											Yes		
Kansas	No													
Kentucky	No											Yes		Yes
Louisiana	No†											Yes		No†
Maine	No											LB		LB
Maryland	Yes	•	•	•	•	•	•	•	•	•		Yes		No
Massachusetts	No	Evaluation team decision										Yes	Pilot Study	Yes
Michigan	No											Yes		No
Minnesota	No											Yes		
Mississippi	No											No	LB	
Missouri	Yes											Yes	LB	LB
Montana	No											LB	LB	LB

Table 4 (Continued)
Summary of NASDSE Survey*
on Competency Testing of Handicapped Children

| State | Mandatory competency test for graduation | Handicaps required for student to take test | | | | | | | | | Special procedures | Regular diplomas | Special diplomas | Certificate of attendance |
		EMR	TMR	LD	SP/Lang	ED	VI	HI	OI	MH				
Nebraska	Yes										Yes	LB	LB	No
Nevada	No											LB	LB	LB
New Hampshire	Yes											LB		Yes
New Jersey	No											Yes		No
New Mexico	Yes											LB	LB	LB
New York	Yes			•	•	•	•	•	•	•	Yes	Yes		No
N. Carolina	Yes											Yes		Yes
N. Dakota	No													LB
Ohio	No											Yes		
Oklahoma	No											Yes		No
Oregon	No											Yes		Yes
Pennsylvania	No											Yes	LB	Yes
Puerto Rico	No											Yes		No
Rhode Island	No											Yes	LB	
S. Carolina	Yes													
S. Dakota	No											LB	LB	LB
Tennessee	Yes 1982											LB	LB	LB
Texas	No											Yes		No
Utah	Yes											Yes	LB	LB
Vermont	Yes	•	•	•	•	•	•	•	•	•	Developing	Yes		No
Virginia	Yes											LB	LB	LB
Washington	No											Yes		No
W. Virginia	No													
Wisconsin	No											LB		LB

*LB, Local board decision; EMR, educable mentally retarded; TMR, trainable mentally retarded; LD, learning disabled; SP/Lang, speech/language; ED, emotionally disturbed; VI, visually impaired; HI, hearing impaired; OI, orthopedically impaired; MH, multihandicapped.
†Local board decision in Orleans parish only.

70 The issuance of regular diplomas also varies among states. Thirty-one states issue regular diplomas to handicapped students. Seventeen states reported that the decision to issue regular diplomas is left to the local school board's discretion. Mississippi did not issue regular diplomas to handicapped students. Special diplomas are issued to handicapped students in Florida. Twelve states reported that they did not issue special diplomas to handicapped students. In 15 states, local school boards decide whether to issue special diplomas.

As indicated in Table 4, certificates of attendance for the handicapped are issued by the District of Columbia and eight states (Florida, Hawaii in 1983, Kentucky, Massachusetts, New Hampshire, North Carolina, Pennsylvania, and Oregon). Certificates of attendance were not issued to the handicapped in 18 states. In 17 states the local board decides whether to issue certificates of attendance to handicapped high school students.

Two additional points need to be made regarding this overview. First, the data presented in Tables 3 and 4 are the most recent available. However, several states have had legislative sessions since the compilation of these data. Some of these legislative bodies have introduced, studied, or changed the policy regarding competency testing in their individual states. Consequently, while these data represent current practices, the situation is probably somewhat different in some states at the time of publication of this article. Second, while some states have not mandated competency testing, individual local education agencies (LEAs)

have made it a policy of their district. For example, Texas does not (at this time) require competency testing. However, the LEA of Austin, Texas, requires that students be assessed for competency. This is probably also true of some of the other school districts throughout the United States.

Although the data presented are not the exact current practices of the states, and some LEA's have their own policies regarding testing, some conclusions can be made. First, there is no consistency regarding the assessment of functional competency throughout the United States. In addition, how the handicapped participate (if at all) in this process also varies considerably. It appears that decisions on these matters are being made more on the basis of local or state philosophy than on any consistent framework for the measurement of functional competency. This should be of considerable concern to parents, educators, and legislators throughout the nation.

LEGAL AND EDUCATIONAL ISSUES

As states began mandating competency testing, two important federal laws also were passed. These laws provided a free appropriate public education in the least restrictive environment for the handicapped student (PL 94-142) and

---

An inherent conflict exists between competency testing requirements and the recent federal laws protecting the handicapped.

---

prohibited discrimination on the basis of handicap in any federally assisted program (Section 504 of the Rehabilitation Act of 1973).

An inherent conflict exists between competency testing requirements and the recent federal laws protecting the handicapped. Competency testing programs are based on the concept that all students should meet a uniform standard of achievement, while PL 94-142 and Section 504 offer assurances of an individualized program to meet varying educational needs. There is a potential for conflict between individualized programs and uniform standards of achievement (McClung & Pullin, 1978; Rosewater, 1979).

Exemption of the handicapped from competency testing is, on the other hand, also in question. Such exemption of the handicapped could be discriminatory by prohibiting some students from full participation in an educational environment that is the least restrictive (McClung & Pullin, 1978; Rosewater, 1979).

McClung (1977) has also pointed out some legal and educational policy issues of competency testing for nonhandicapped students. These include (a) potential for racial discrimination in the selection and administration of specific measures, (b) inadequate advance notice and phase-in periods prior to the initial use of the tests, (c) possible lack of validity and reliability of the instruments used, (d) inadequate match between what is taught in the schools and what is tested on the measures, (e) for students who fail the test, remedial instruction that may be inadequate or may reinforce tracking, and (f) unfair apportionment of responsibility for test failure between students and teachers.

Special educators should carefully analyze the references previously cited in this section—they are key writings for those concerned with measuring functional competencies in both the handicapped and nonhandicapped populations. One fundamental question that special educators must address is how mandated testing programs can be implemented so that opportunity for the handicapped student is consistent with the requirements of PL 94-142 and Section 504. This requires a translation of predominantly legal constraints into educational practices.

RECOMMENDATIONS

The authors believe there are two approaches to assessment of functional competency of the handicapped that have merit. The first approach applies to those personnel who must immediately begin testing for competency. These professionals should develop a written rationale or philosophy for the measurement of functional competency of the handicapped. Basically this rationale should answer questions on the purpose of testing. For example, is the handicapped student being tested for the purpose of improving his or her educational program, providing an opportunity for participation in the least restrictive environment, determining whether a greater variety of teaching techniques needs to be used, or determining whether a school program is meeting its obligations to educate its students? The

72

answers to these and other questions should provide a basis for determining whether a handicapped student should participate in the testing program. The committee that determines the individualized educational program can use the rationale to delineate the type of involvement most appropriate for a particular student. This process should provide an opportunity for most students and their parents to specify the type and amount of participation in the competency testing program for each handicapped individual.

The authors feel more comfortable in recommending the repeal of all legislation that mandates competency testing for any student (either handicapped or nonhandicapped). A review of the literature has pointed out the following aspects of the current state of the art on functional competency testing:

- The construct itself is not well understood.
- The terms used to describe this construct vary as well as their definitions.
- There are considerable differences throughout the United States regarding the policies and practices in assessment of both handicapped and nonhandicapped students.
- Some individual states' legal and educational practices relative to competency testing and the handicapped may conflict with PL 94-142 and Section 504.

It is inappropriate for decisions to be made regarding a person's competency and the issuance of a diploma until data are available demonstrating that such decisions have social and educational benefits.

Finally, the authors recognize that their recommendation that all laws be repealed will have little effect. Many, probably most, readers will dismiss these observations as the impractical thoughts of academicians and parents. For the most part, legislators will continue to pass laws and educators will continue to implement policies regarding competency testing. Eventually, however, the schools will most likely be sued by irate parents, minority groups, and students themselves. With the state of the art regarding assessment of functional competency being what it is, it is unlikely that the schools will have a defensible case.

REFERENCES

Bormuth, J. R. Reading literacy: Its definitions and assessment. *Reading Research Quarterly*, 1975, *74*, 7-66.

Buchanan, D. W. Two visions of literacy. *English Quarterly*, 1975, *10*, 73-75.

Cook, W. *Adult literacy education in the U.S.* Newark, Del.: International Reading Association, 1977.

Dauzat, S. V., & Dauzat, J. A. Literacy: In quest of a definition. *Adult Literacy and Basic Education*, 1977, *1*, 1-5.

Davis, R. G. Needed: Functional literacy skills, curricula and tests. *Educational Technology*, 1977, *17*, 52-54.

Elgin, S. H. The real literacy crisis. *Change*, 1978, *10*, 10-11.

Florida Bureau of Education for Exceptional Students. *A resource manual for the development and evaluation of programs for exceptional students.* Tallahassee, Fla.: Florida Department of Education, 1978.

Grattan, C. *American ideas about adult education.* New York: Teachers College, Columbia University, 1959.

Harman, D. Illiteracy: An overview. *Harvard Education Review*, 1970, *2*, 226-243.

Kerlinger, F. N. *Behavioral research: A conceptual approach.* New York: Holt, Rinehart & Winston, 1979.

Larson, C. A. Problems in assessing functional communication. *Communication Education*, 1978, *27*, 304-309.

Lieb-Brilhart, B. What if Johnny could read and write?. . . Another look at the literacy issue. *Communication Education*, 1977, *26*, 251-253.

Linde, J. C. *Competency testing, special education and the awarding of diplomas.* Washington, D. C.: National Association of State Directors of Special Education, 1979.

McClung, M. S. Competency testing: Potential for discrimination. *Clearinghouse Review*, 1977, 439-448.

McClung, M. S., & Pullin, D. Competency testing and handicapped students. *Clearinghouse Review*, 1978, 922-927.

Miller, G. A. *Linguistic communication: Perspectives for research.* Newark, Del.: National Reading Council, 1973.

Murphy, R. T. Assessment of adult reading competence. In D. M. Neilsen & H. F. Hjelm (Eds.), *Reading and career education.* Newark, Del.: International Reading Association, 1975.

Northcutt, N. W. Functional literacy for adults. In D. M. Neilsen & H. F. Hjelm (Eds.), *Reading and career education.* Newark, Del.: International Reading Association, 1975.

Norton, J. R. Back-to-basics and student minimal competency evaluation: How to spell "school" with three R's and an E. *Contemporary Education*, 1979, *50*, 98-103.

Pipho, C. State activity: Minimal competency testing. Denver: Education Commission of the States, 1979.

Powell, W. R. Levels of literacy. *Journal of Reading*, 1977, *20*, 488-492.

Robinson, H. A. Libraries: Active agents in adult reading improvement. *American Library Association Bulletin*, 1963, *57*, 416-421.

Rosewater, A. *Minimum competency testing programs and handicapped students: Perspectives on policy and practice.* Washington, D.C.: Institute for Educational Leadership, 1979.

Smith, L. L. Literacy: Definitions and implications. *Language Arts*, 1977, *54*, 135-138.

Sticht, T. G. *Reading for working.* Alexandria, Va.: Human Resources Research Organization, 1975.

Wiemann, J. M. Needed research and training in speaking and listening literacy. *Communication Education*, 1978, *27*, 310-315.

A Conceptual Framework for Assessment of Curriculum and Student Progress

Mary Poplin
University of Kansas Medical Center
Kansas City, Kansas

Richard Gray
University of Oklahoma
Norman, Oklahoma

WORDS AND PHRASES certain to arouse rounds of applause and nods of agreement from today's educators include *individualization, assessment for instruction,* and *specially designed programs to meet unique needs,* among others of similar meaning to special educators. Of less certainty, especially in actual practice, are answers to questions such as (a) Who should be responsible for the assessment? (b) Who is best suited to conduct the assessment and design of individualized programs? and (c) How can one be assured that both the assessment and the educational program resulting from that assessment are appropriate and meaningful?

The authors contend that classroom teachers are best suited to assess students' progress because (a) they have unequaled knowledge of the student and the goals most necessary to his or her life, (b) they have continual contact with the child in

0196-6960/80/0013-0075$2.00

76 the classroom, and (c) student progress is ultimately their primary concern. Therefore teachers, rather than diagnostic, psychometric, or supervisory personnel, should have the primary responsibility for assessment of student needs and progress. The authors also believe that many, if not most, teachers now perform the informal assessments that are the most relevant, regardless of the edicts of school district policy or state and federal regulations.

The following discussion of assessment is directed to the special teachers and, to a lesser extent, to school administrators and other decision makers who design systems for assessment of student progress in the schools. The intent is to discuss a conceptual framework that will facilitate appropriate, meaningful, and efficient educational instruction and assessment of student progress toward meeting life-related goals and objectives. Because good informal classroom assessment activities are virtually synonymous with good classroom instruction, the stages presented apply to instruction as well as to the design and implementation of efficient informal assessments.

Assessment is the key to appropriate instruction. For classroom purposes, assessment performed for any other reason is without meaning (Wallace & Larsen, 1978). Regardless of fine phrases such as "instruction designed to meet unique needs," assessment of a student is based on the assessor's perceptions of what is important and on predetermined curricula imposed by school systems, publishers, and "experts." Effectiveness in instruction and assessment is directly re-

lated to the teacher's intuitive or learned understanding of the following: (a) functional, life-related needs and goals for the education of each individual; (b) instructional content that best incorporates those goals; (c) development of curriculum designed to achieve these goals; and (d) instructional strategies used to systematically teach and assess student progress. Combined, these elements are the guiding force in both instruction and the assessment of student progress.

The implication is this: the appropriateness of any curriculum depends on the effectiveness of a teacher in meeting its objectives, and meaningful assessment of student progress depends on appropriate use of the curriculum. The most appropriate curriculum is that curriculum designed by the teacher(s) responsible for its implementation. Therefore an important teaching skill is the teacher's willingness and ability to design and continuously evaluate the curriculum as it is being implemented in the classroom. Only when the curriculum is continuously evaluated can any direct student assessment be considered valid.

STAGES OF ASSESSMENT

Two stages are necessary for teachers to conduct effective assessment: *stage 1*—continuous evaluation or assessment of the curriculum being implemented to help students achieve life-related goals; and *stage 2*—direct assessment of student performance within that curriculum through the careful structuring and observation of instructional strategies.

Stage 1: Teacher Assessment of Educational Curricula

Informal assessment or evaluation of curricula for exceptional learners accomplishes several purposes. First, and perhaps most important, it allows teachers to continually design, select, modify, and change goals and objectives for individual students on the basis of their best professional judgment rather than on the edicts of the school administration, the latest educational fads, or the latest commercially produced curriculum materials. Second, it gives teachers a greater awareness of, as well as a greater control over, what is happening to students whose education is their responsibility. Third, through continuous design, redesign, and evaluation of a curriculum one obtains greater flexibility in applying information obtained from direct assessment of students in the classroom to other educational environments; that is, instructional objectives and strategies can be selected on the basis of knowledge of the student's previous educational background and present life circumstances. Figure 1 presents a model to facilitate the evaluation of curriculum from the teacher's perspective.

Figure 1. Stage of Informal Assessment: A Model for the Classification of Educational Curriculum

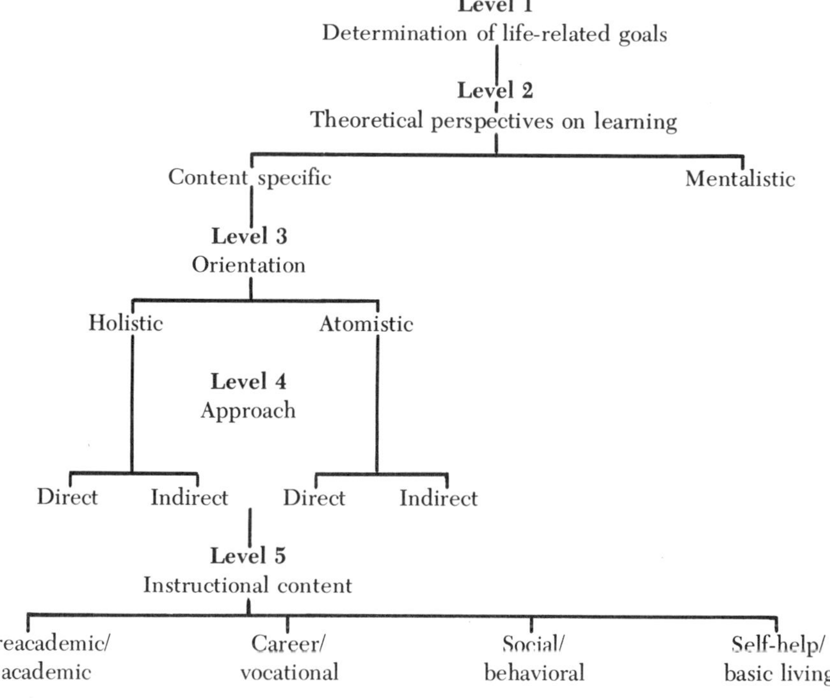

Adapted from Hammill, D. D., Brown, L. L., Brown, V. L., Gray, R. A., Hresko, W. P., Larsen, S. C., McNutt, G., Poplin, M. S., Reid, D. K., & Wiederholt, J. L. A model for classifying instructional strategies. Unpublished manuscript, University of Oklahoma, 1979.

78

LEVEL 1: DETERMINATION OF LIFE-RELATED GOALS

The danger of using a predetermined curriculum as the basis for assessment and instructional programming, no matter how sound its rationale, is that the curriculum becomes the master; the child's needs are seen only in terms of what the curriculum has to offer. The only content suitable as a basis for effective assessment and instruction results from a comparison of the child's present abilities and the abilities and understanding necessary for a satisfying, self-fulfilling life.

The most meaningful long-range life goals include independent functioning in adult society—that is, the ability to (a) interact effectively and appropriately with family, friends, and coworkers; (b) support oneself financially; (c) find satisfaction in both work and leisure; and (d) have options and make satisfying decisions regarding career, marriage, social life, and civic participation.

More immediate life goals, albeit often less meaningful ones to the student, are those skills that allow functioning in the social system imposed by the school environment—for example, to stay in one's chair, perform well on worksheets, wait or walk in line, and follow other rules and conventions of the classroom. The teacher is the most important person in determining these life-related goals and thus in

---

The danger of using a predetermined curriculum as the basis for assessment and instructional programming . . . is that the curriculum becomes the master.

---

structuring curricula to fill these needs. Often, special educators are aware of the differences in what is required for successful adult functioning and what is demanded for successful school functioning. This awareness, painful as it often is, requires teachers to juggle lifelong and school-related goals into an amalgamated, yet appropriate, curriculum. The current trend in mainstreaming the handicapped child into the regular classroom has made this task of combining long-range and immediate life goals an even more arduous one.

LEVEL 2: THEORETICAL PERSPECTIVES ON LEARNING

Once teachers have determined life-related goals, they must clarify their own theoretical perspectives on learning that will be apparent in their curricula. Teachers can take one of two major theoretical perspectives on learning: content specific or mentalistic.

Content-specific curriculum deals directly with instruction and assessment of life-related goals. All activities and knowledge directed to or discovered by students should be clearly relevant to the skills and abilities they will need to function adequately in life. Reading instruction will center on reading experiences rather than underlying processes thought to be related to reading. Writing instruction will center on expressing ideas through writing rather than hypothetical psychological processes presumed to underlie the ability to write, such as perceptual skills.

In an adaptation of a working paper to propose a model for classifying and analyzing approaches to instruction, Hammill, Brown, L.L., Brown, V.L., Gray, Hresko, Larsen, McNutt, Poplin, Reid, and Wiederholt (1979) suggested two major approaches to education: the educational content approach (as described previously) and the mentalistic process approach, in which presumed psychological prerequisite functions are trained to facilitate content and skill acquisition. The authors point out that research does not support such a mentalistic process approach at this time. We agree with this observation and have chosen not to deal further with mentalistic process curriculum, as indicated by Figure 1 (see Mann, 1980, for further discussion of process training).

LEVEL 3: ORIENTATION TO EDUCATION

At a third level, teachers must evaluate whether the orientation to their curriculum is holistic or atomistic. The holistic orientation assumes that instruction involves structuring the educational environment to provide students with experiences that will allow them to assimilate new meanings, skills, relationships, and insights into their present knowledge. This assimilation will, in the context of a relevant instructional environment, develop into systems of useful skills and information. Children learn through practical, self-selected experiences in a carefully arranged environment.

The atomistic orientation, in contrast, assumes that the steps for learning skills and content areas are known, that rules must be taught, and that systematic presentation of the steps and rules will add up to mastery of the specific whole—the skill or specific content area. In this orientation, content, steps, and sequence are predetermined and imposed. Children learn through direct instruction in specific component skills.

The authors believe that the most appropriate orientation generally is holistic; however, it is necessary for teachers to have a full understanding of the skills involved in any content area to facilitate student progress in meeting the chosen life-related goals. We also recognize the possibility that some educational goals or objectives may be most efficiently met through an atomistic approach or that atomistic learning may sometimes precede holistic assimilation (see Vygotsky's 1962 discussion of the development of spontaneous versus scientific concepts).

LEVEL 4: APPROACH TO INSTRUCTION

Teachers who design and assess curriculum are also aware of the various approaches possible to the instruction of content-specific material. Some curricula are designed to instruct students specifically in the life-related goals. These curricula use the direct approach. Other curricula are generated to teach strategies or skills that hopefully will transfer and generalize so that life-related skills are more easily attainable. These curricula take the indirect approach.

However, both of these approaches deal with educational *content* as opposed to mentalistic *processes*. For example, curricula that are designed to teach students study skills from an indirect approach deemphasize the content of the social studies or science materials being used. The assumption is that students

80

who have acquired certain study skills or strategies will be able to more efficiently learn and understand the social studies or science materials. Teachers using a direct instructional approach design curriculum that contains the specific content to be learned by the students. The differences between these two approaches result in considerable variations in curricula.

LEVEL 5: INSTRUCTIONAL CONTENT

As indicated in Figure 1, the content of life-related goals is clustered under four headings: preacademic/academic, career/vocational, social/behavioral, and self-help/basic living skills. It is at this level that teaching strategies are important in the curriculum and that decisions made at previous levels are put into operation.

IMPORTANCE OF CURRICULUM ASSESSMENT

The importance of teachers' informally assessing their own curricula during the first stage of pupil assessment cannot be overstated. Unless teachers intuitively understand and are free to choose and change their kinds of curriculum, they are merely automatons of some large system that dictates their teaching. In addition, unless teachers understand their own curriculum perspectives, direct pupil assessment will be vague and without meaning.

The first stage of pupil assessment must therefore be assessment of the educational curriculum with attention given to the determination or designation of life-related goals (level 1), the theoretical perspective on learning held by individual teachers (content specific or mentalistic, level 2), the general orientation to education (holistic or atomistic, level 3), the ap-

proach to instruction considered most viable (direct or indirect, level 4), and the content of instruction (level 5). Unfortunately, with the exception of level 2, there is little research that clearly guides the choices of teachers of handicapped individuals. Once the life-related curriculum has been established and clarified, teachers can begin the direct informal assessment of student progress in meeting educational goals and objectives (stage 2).

Stage 2: Direct Assessment of Student Progress

The second stage of informal assessment requires a more specific model, one that examines actual classroom *instructional strategies* and allows the teacher to assess student progress within the curriculum. This stage is closely related to level 5 of the model for classification of educational curriculum (Figure 1). Instructional strategies are defined as the interaction between educational objectives and classroom activities. This fusion of educational objectives and classroom activities fills virtually every instructional day and produces what are commonly called "instructional objectives." The model presented here is an attempt to provide a simple, efficient framework from which teachers can assess student progress in meeting various educational objectives within the context of classroom activities. The model also provides a way of explaining, examining, and structuring curriculum.

A model that allows for specific inspection of instructional strategies (i.e., educational objectives and classroom activities) accomplishes several purposes. First—and most critical to this discussion—is that the model of curriculum allows educators to develop appropriate means or activities for informally assessing student performance in given educational objectives. Inherent in this purpose is the advantage of being able to consciously designate a particular activity as representing mastery of that objective. Second, it allows teachers to evaluate classroom activities in terms of the objective(s) to be met. Thus teachers using this model are also stimulated to make conscientious decisions regarding classroom activities based on the awareness of alternatives and the even more acute awareness of which activities constitute mastery of specified goals. Third, both models or stages can guide and stimulate the much-needed research into the acquisition of knowledge by providing a classification structure for the various kinds of classroom activities that are presently planned.

Figure 2 is designed to provide structure for the above purposes; however, central to this discussion is that the model will direct teachers in the development and execution of informal assessments of student progress toward the mastery of educational objectives. The two-dimensional model depicts the interaction between classroom activities and educational objectives (i.e., the level of the curriculum that is used to assess students' progress).

CLASSROOM ACTIVITIES

Classroom activities have been categorized into two distinct types of actions: *natural* and *synthetic* (created purely for instructional purposes). To determine whether an assessment activity is synthetic or natural, one must consider the goal or activity that would constitute mastery. For example, if the ultimate goal or mastery of the activity is that a student

Figure 2. A Model of Instructional Strategies for the Informal Assessment of Student Progress

CLASSROOM ACTIVITY	EDUCATIONAL OBJECTIVE	
	Mechanical	Conceptual
Natural		
Synthetic		

82

use the appropriate punctuation marks at the ends of sentences, but the assessment activity requires that the student rewrite a given sentence correctly, circle errors, or punctuate given sentences, then the activity is synthetic. The activity has been synthetically created and artificially imposed on the student for instructional purposes. In contrast, if the student writes a composition and the teacher notes end-mark punctuation errors and abilities, the assessment activity would be considered natural. Teachers conduct natural assessments by observing the student in the actual activity required for mastery of the objective. Synthetic assessment activities are manufactured within a highly structured, artificial setting.

The advantage of synthetic activities is that observation or assessment is made uniform across students and situations and thus is simplified. Standardized instruments are almost exclusively synthetic because of the necessity to standardize (make reliable and valid) and simplify scoring and to sample large numbers of educational objectives in relatively short periods of time. Synthetic activities, including both formal and informal assessment activities, are far more common than natural activities in most school curricula.

The disadvantage of synthetic activities is that they do not provide students the chance to practice, nor teachers the opportunity to observe, mastery of a given educational objective in a real-life situation. Unfortunately there is also a serious lack of research that answers such questions as whether (or to what degree) syn-

Synthetic activities . . . do not provide students the chance to practice, nor teachers the opportunity to observe, mastery of a given educational objective in a real-life situation.

thetic activities promote mastery of given educational objectives in natural settings.

Natural activities and assessment are more life-related activities and offer a different set of advantages. The most obvious advantage is, of course, that they allow the student an opportunity to apply and practice certain skills or objectives within their natural context. Thus there is little or no question that the objective can be accomplished when and where needed. A concomitant advantage is that generalization to other settings (e.g., the use of appropriate end marks in letter writing and social studies reports) would be more likely to occur.

The disadvantages of natural activities are the primary reason for the scarcity of such activities and assessments in today's classrooms. By the nature of such activities, assessment must be conducted through careful observation. This observation often involves both observation of the process or operation while the student performs the activity, and careful analysis of the resultant product. Products of natural activities are highly individual rather than uniform, making the analysis even more difficult. Of course, the time and adaptability of the teacher required for natural assessments and activities are tremendous.

These added burdens obviously are discouraging to teachers of handicapped children who are already inundated with individual differences, not to mention the paperwork demands of special education today (see Katzen, 1980). However, natural activities and assessments may be even more important for students with problems than for ordinary students. The "normal" student may make rapid generalizations from synthetic activities and transfer these skills to other settings much more readily than handicapped learners. Regardless, both synthetic and natural activities and assessments comprise one dimension of instructional strategies, that is, classroom activities.

EDUCATIONAL OBJECTIVES

The second dimension of the model of instructional strategies represents the two primary types of educational objectives: *mechanical* and *conceptual*. Mechanical objectives are those objectives or skills that require learning by rote facts, rules, or principles, the sequential operation of a series of related tasks, or the systematic application of these skills within the contexts of certain situations. The addition of two three-digit numerals is a skill that can be acquired mechanically and applied in several settings, as can the appropriate use of end-mark punctuation.

While these mechanical skills can often be generalized or transferred to other settings through specific instruction, generalization and transfer abilities are far more uncertain than with conceptual objectives. However, an educational objective that is conceptual demands that the student understand intuitively the reasons behind various mechanical performances, allowing for more flexibility,

generalization, and transfer to occur. The student who has acquired the conceptual objective of three-digit addition understands the principles of place value, set union, and numerosity, among others. A student may, however, intuitively understand the *concept* of place value and not know the mechanics of reciting the rules or even the label for such a principle.

Another example of the differences between conceptual and mechanical objectives is apparent in spoken language differences. A student from one cultural background may not use the plural *s* at the end of words. This in no way indicates that the child imagines only one animal when he or she says "Three dog got in a fight." Another student with more conceptual language disorders may be taught the mechanics of adding *s* to nouns following certain numbers of objects but may not actually understand the concept of "more than one."

Many educational objectives stated or observed in the classroom are mechanical rather than conceptual. Mechanical objectives (i.e., the production of rote rules, facts, and principles or the sequential production of certain motions) involve activities that are more easily designed, instituted, and assessed. In addition, teachers find mechanical objectives easy to define into readily observed tasks, thus more conducive to assessments using behavioral technology. True conceptual objectives are not so readily taught or assessed by using a task analysis and reinforcement technology because they are not easily broken into individual tasks and subtasks and require both integration and assimilation by students. Providing stu-

84

dents with a multitude of concrete experiences such as those discussed by Piagetian and Brunerian scholars seems the most appropriate means for both the instruction and observation of those objectives. Progress toward conceptual objectives must be assessed through a long series of fairly complex and often subjective observations of the students interacting within their various environments. Mechanical as well as conceptual objectives are necessary in all good classroom curricula; both must be assessed in thorough, informal evaluations of student progress.

INSTRUCTIONAL STRATEGIES IN ASSESSMENT

The instructional strategies that result from the interaction of educational objectives and classroom activities provide the structure for designing appropriate informal assessment activities. To demonstrate the dynamics of this interaction as it relates to classroom assessment, several examples are offered. General or educational objectives from the areas of math computation, written expression-punctuation, math concepts, and self-help skills are used in the following comparisons. *General objectives* is the term given a specific format for designing educational objectives proposed by Poplin (1979) and Larsen and Poplin (1980). This particular format was proposed to bridge the gap between educational goals and short-term instructional objectives created by the requirements of PL 94-142.

Figure 3 illustrates instructional strategies that might be used to assess student progress in selected general objectives. Of particular note is the manner in which each objective is assessed with the use of both synthetic and natural activities. The following general objectives are used as examples in Figure 3:

- Addition of decimal numerals;
- End-mark punctuation;
- Sight word vocabulary (level N Dolch);
- Concept of bigger, larger, smaller, greater than, less than; and
- Drinking from cup.

By their nature, some general objectives will be either mechanical or conceptual. For example, "end-mark punctuation" is a mechanical skill, while "greater than, less than" is a conceptual objective. Therefore not every general objective can be assessed conceptually and mechanically. However, together the conceptual objectives involved in sentence construction and the mechanical skills of punctuation result in a major step toward the goal of natural and independent written expression.

Research does not indicate whether worksheet decimal addition in any way aids or enhances the learning of the concept of the decimal system and its application to addition (see discussion by Cawley, Fitzmaurice, Shaw, Kahn, & Bates, 1978). It is probably true that the closer one is to the natural mechanics and conceptual activities, the closer one is to achieving the ultimate goal or objective. It appears from the examples that perhaps the least valuable or most questionable are those synthetic conceptual activities. These appear to be far removed from the mechanical or conceptual abilities that are ultimately the goal, although they certainly are expedient classroom activities.

Figure 3. Examples of Instructional Strategies Used for Informal Assessment of Objectives

<table>
<tr><td colspan="2" rowspan="2"></td><td colspan="2" align="center">EDUCATIONAL OBJECTIVES</td></tr>
<tr><td align="center">Mechanical</td><td align="center">Conceptual</td></tr>
<tr><td rowspan="10" align="center">CLASSROOM ACTIVITIES</td><td rowspan="5" align="center">Natural</td><td>Adds own lunch bill without aids.</td><td>Shows addition of decimals by estimating and summing amounts owed or received.</td></tr>
<tr><td>Uses appropriate end-mark punctuation in originally composed sentences.</td><td></td></tr>
<tr><td>Reads aloud level N Dolch words when presented in contextual reading materials.</td><td>Silently reads a selection containing Dolch words and summarizes contents of selection.</td></tr>
<tr><td></td><td>Chooses the larger or smaller group of objects when needed.</td></tr>
<tr><td>Asks for "cup" when thirsty.</td><td>Uses "cups" of all dimensions when thirsty.</td></tr>
<tr><td rowspan="5" align="center">Synthetic</td><td>Adds decimal numbers on a worksheet.</td><td>Solves story problems involving the addition of decimal numbers.</td></tr>
<tr><td>Rewrites a given sentence and supplies missing end-mark punctuation.</td><td></td></tr>
<tr><td>Names aloud level N Dolch words when shown in isolation.</td><td>Chooses correct Dolch words from a multiple-choice format to complete a given sentence.</td></tr>
<tr><td></td><td>Places "greater than" and "less than" signs in a list of digit pairs ($<$　$>$).</td></tr>
<tr><td>Says "cup" when presented a picture or object.</td><td>Selects all containers that could be cups from a picture or set of objects.</td></tr>
</table>

86

These are but a few examples of the ways in which teachers can design and implement informed assessment activities using this model. The model also provides teachers with a way of monitoring instructional and assessment strategies taking place in their classrooms, allowing them once again to make conscientious and informed decisions.

• • •

Both stages of assessment—teachers' assessment of their own curriculum theories, orientations, and approaches, and direct assessment of students through use of strategies that incorporate both mechanical and conceptual objectives in natural or synthetic settings—are necessary for the efficient assessment of student progress. Both stages involve assessment that can be done efficiently only by the special teacher who is daily responsible for the handicapped learner's program.

REFERENCES

Cawley, J. F., Fitzmaurice, A. M., Shaw, R. A., Kahn, H., & Bates, H. Mathematics and learning disabled youth: The upper grade levels. *Learning Disabilities Quarterly*, 1978, *1*, 37-52.

Hammill, D. D., Brown, L. L., Brown, V. L., Gray, R. A., Hresko, W. P., Larsen, S. C., McNutt, G., Poplin, M. S., Reid, D. K., & Wiederholt, J. L. A model for classifying instructional strategies. Unpublished manuscript, University of Oklahoma, 1979.

Katzen, K. To the editor: An open letter to CEC. *Exceptional Children*, 1980, *46*, 582.

Larsen, S. C., & Poplin, M. S. *Methods for educating the handicapped*. Boston: Allyn & Bacon, 1980.

Mann, L. *On the trail of process: A historical perspective on cognitive processes and their training*. New York: Grune & Stratton, 1980.

Poplin, M. S. The science of curriculum development applied to special education and the IEP. *Focus on Exceptional Children*, 1979, *12*(3), 1-16.

Vygotsky, L. S. *Thought and language*. Cambridge, Mass.: The MIT Press, 1962.

Wallace, G. & Larsen, S. C. *Educational assessment of learning problems*. Boston: Allyn & Bacon, 1978.

Assessment of Severely and Profoundly Handicapped Individuals

Susan Johnsen Dollar
Educational Consultant
Austin, Texas

Carol Brooks
University of Kentucky
Lexington, Kentucky

ONE OF THE SMALLEST defined subgroups in special education is that of severely and profoundly handicapped (SPH) individuals. Depending on the type of handicapping condition considered, prevalence estimates have ranged between 0.1% and 0.9% of the general population (Kauffman & Payne, 1975; Mercer, 1975). For many years SPH children often received little more than custodial care owing to their low incidence and a prevailing attitude among some professionals of their ineducability (Haring & Pious, 1976). With the concerns of the 1960s toward individual constitutional rights, the 1970s litigation decisions toward a zero-reject educational model, and the passage of subsequent legislation, public and professional views began to change. PL 94-142 set service priorities for children with the "most severe handicaps within each disability area" receiving an "inadequate education." This legislative mandate raised im-

88

portant questions related to the area of assessment:

- What criteria should be used in identifying children with the most severe handicaps?
- What criteria should be used in assessing the adequacy of SPH programs?
- How might educational assessment of SPH children differ from other special educational populations?

This article addresses each of these assessment issues.

ASSESSMENT FOR IDENTIFICATION

To ensure that children with the most severe handicaps received appropriate services, criteria for identification needed to be developed. The Bureau of Education for the Handicapped (1974) described this population by publishing the following definition:

> Severely handicapped children are those who because of the intensity of their physical, mental, or emotional problems, need educational, social, psychological, and medical services beyond those which are traditionally offered by regular and special education programs, in order to maximize participation in society and self-fulfillment. Such severely handicapped children may possess severe language or perceptual-cognitive deprivations and evidence a number of abnormal behaviors including failure to attend to even the most pronounced stimuli, self-mutilation, manifestations of durable and intense temper tantrums, and the absence of even the most rudimentary forms of verbal control. They may also have extremely fragile physiological conditions.

This definition delineates three essential characteristics in identifying SPH children: (a) they must have a "severe" or "intense" handicap; (b) they need an educational program requiring greater resources than are normally provided by traditional programs; and (c) they need programs that focus on skills necessary for greater independent functioning and "self-fulfillment." Because the handicap may occur in the physical, mental, or emotional areas, the SPH population may include children with such diverse labels as autistic, cerebral palsied, deaf-blind, mentally retarded, multiply handicapped, schizophrenic, and learning disabled.

Determining Severity

Numerous attempts have been made by universities, state departments, and local school systems to define the SPH population. While current definitions vary in the use of general or behavioral terms, all include a reference to the degree of the handicapping condition (e.g., "extremely brittle," "intense," "serious," "severe," "profound"). The nature of norm-referenced classification systems required special educators to address the problem of differentiating the severely handicapped from other special education groups. The significant question became: How severe is severe?

The most frequently used criterion for severity is performance four standard deviations or more below the mean (Bricker, Dubose, Alberte, Berkler, Filler, Gast, Holder, Jens, Kauffman, Sears, & Snell,

1978). Problems with this criterion relate to the norm group used and the standardization process itself. First, SPH children are not included or are not adequately represented in most norming samples. Lack of inclusion is often due to the small number of SPH children available. For this reason, most test manuals fail to describe norms or include many items below the third or fourth standard deviation, where most SPH children perform. Second, the severely and profoundly handicapped population is extremely heterogeneous. Even if a representative sample for each subgroup were included, the small number would not be appropriate for standardization purposes. Third, standardized tests require controlled conditions for any valid comparison. Again, the diversity among SPH children and the severity of their handicaps often require a modification of the test instrument itself (i.e., many SPH children lack the necessary communication skills required by most tests).

Aware of the lack of "precision" of most norm-referenced tests, Bricker and Iacino (1977) have used consensus between observers in determining severity. They have found "considerable agreement" in "what constitutes a significant deficiency or impairment" (p. 168).

SPH children are not included or are not adequately represented in most norming samples. . . often due to the small number of SPH children available.

Other professionals have focused on the rate at which new behaviors are acquired as a better indicator of a "severe" deficiency (McKenzie, Hill, Sousie, York, & Baker, 1977). In this model a minimum set of objectives for each developmental year is specified. A minimum rate line is then determined by the number of objectives a child would need to achieve each year to make normal progress. If a child "falls below the minimum rate line for achievement of the birth-to-two-year span of minimum objectives, s/he is eligible for SPH programs" (p. 101).

These latter approaches to identification (i.e., observer consensus and minimum rate) may be more valid and reliable for SPH children than norm-referenced tests. However, early identification is often facilitated by the SPH child's marked physical abnormalities or unresponsiveness to environmental stimuli. It may be more important to develop and use identification procedures that are easy to administer by available personnel to ensure the implementation of "wide-scale screening" and early intervention (Haring, 1976).

Determining "Greater" Resources

The SPH child often presents a multiplicity of handicaps, requiring services beyond the "traditional" school program. Physicians, physical and occupational therapists, audiologists, psychologists, speech clinicians, social workers, and highly trained teachers are often needed to assess the child's current level of functioning and plan his or her educational program.

90

In addition, the SPH child needs these specialized services for longer periods of time than other children. Bricker and Iacino (1977) have described this type of needed intervention as "longitudinal" as opposed to "episodic." A less "severe" child may require only temporary medical assistance in controlling seizures or short-term physical therapy sessions in developing motor control while the SPH child will need continued assistance. Using this criterion, children who need an episodic intervention would not be eligible for services provided by an SPH program.

Determining Areas for Programming

Given that SPH children have deficits equal to or greater than four standard deviations below the mean, they will need an educational program that focuses on skills leading to greater independent functioning (Brown, Nietupski, & Hamre-Nietupski, 1976). Sailor and Haring (1977) have described these skills as "basic" as opposed to "academic." Using this criterion, children who need academic instruction would not be referred to an SPH program.

In summary, children must meet three criteria to be eligible for SPH programs:

1. They must have a "severe" handicap. Severity may be determined by norm-referenced tests (a score four standard deviations or more below the mean), agreement between observers (Bricker & Iacino, 1977), or learning rate curves (McKenzie et al., 1977).

2. They need greater resources than normally provided within traditional pro-grams. In addition, these resources are needed on a long-term basis (i.e., longitudinal intervention) (Bricker & Iacino, 1977).

3. They need basic skill development that will lead to greater independent functioning in society or to "self-fulfillment." Because the identification of SPH children is often facilitated by their marked abnormalities or unresponsiveness to environmental stimuli, screening procedures should be efficient and readily accessible to available professionals so that all SPH children receive services at as early an age as possible.

ASSESSMENT FOR EDUCATIONAL PROGRAMMING

Besides identifying children eligible for service, the other major purpose of assessment is to provide the teacher with the information necessary for planning and evaluating each child's educational program. Assessment instruments used in educational programming should (a) be able to measure the child's current level of functioning so the teacher will know where to begin, (b) have items that are sequenced in a logical hierarchy so the teacher will know what to teach next, (c) describe the testing conditions in which the child performed at an optimal level so the teacher can create the optimum learning environment, and (d) identify criteria used for acceptable performance so the teacher will know when the student is ready to proceed to the next skill. Tests possessing these characteristics have been identified as the "cornerstone for systematic instruction," uniting "testing with teaching" (Dubose, 1978, p. 9).

The need for special educators to examine whether tests used with other special education populations are appropriate in planning and evaluating SPH programs was mentioned earlier. To evaluate these instruments and also provide programming information for the SPH child, professionals have focused on developing criteria for each of the following areas: item content, item sequence, assessment conditions, and mastery criteria.

Item Content

Two criteria are generally used in determining content areas for SPH assessment and programming: basic behaviors and ultimate functioning. Basic behaviors are those that relate to areas producing greater independence (e.g., self-help, communication). The "criterion of ultimate functioning" means that the task must be one a child might encounter in the "natural" environment (Brown et al., 1976). Consequently item content should be ascertained by observing skills necessary for living and adapting within the immediate community. Any test that measures only academic behaviors would be inappropriate for the SPH population.

Sailor and Haring (1977) have identified the following functional domains from a developmental viewpoint: self-help, sensory-motor, communication, and social skills. Others have developed domains from a remedial or age-appropriate standpoint (Brown, Branston, Nietupski, Pumpian, Certo, & Gruenewald, 1979; Guess, Horner, Utley, Holvoet, Maxon, Tucker, & Warren, 1978). Their curricula include domestic living, vocational training, leisure and recreation time, and community functioning. In addition, competing behaviors (e.g., self-abuse or stereotypic behaviors) often must be eliminated first before the SPH child is ready to learn how to attend or respond to the task situation. Most tests developed and standardized with SPH populations assess these domain areas. Exceptions are tests that focus on a limited age span (i.e., infant scales) or a specific disability (e.g., visual efficiency).

TEST VARIATIONS

Variations between tests tend to occur in (a) the number of behaviors or skills listed under each domain and (b) the organization of these domains. For example, the TARC System (Topeka Association for Retarded Citizens) (Sailor & Mix, 1975) contains 108 behavioral descriptions organized into four domains, which are further divided into 12 subdomains; the American Association on Mental Deficiency Adaptive Behavior Scale (ABS) (Nihira, Foster, Shellhaas, & Leland, 1974) contains approximately 315 behavioral descriptions, organized into two parts divided into 24 domains and 18 subdomains. The number of items is partly determined by whether the test is intended to be used for only screening or for a more comprehensive assessment (i.e., the more comprehensive the instrument, the more test items). In this manner, Sailor and Haring (1977) have described the TARC as a position I system (i.e., screening instrument) and the ABS as a position III system (i.e., comprehensive).

91

92 However, even within the same level systems there are differences. For example, the Behavioral Characteristics Progression (BCP) (Office of the Santa Cruz County Superintendent of Schools, 1973) and the ABS are both identified as level III systems. Yet the BCP contains 59 strands, whereas the ABS contains 24 domains. These differences are often due to the conceptualization of different domains or strands. Factor analytic studies of part I of the ABS have identified three domains from the original 11 subdomains (Nihira, 1978). The three new major domains included personal self-sufficiency, community self-sufficiency, and personal-social responsibility.

TEACHER'S STANDPOINT

Because teachers often use tests in determining what to teach within the classroom situation, it may be important to view content organization from a teaching standpoint. Williams and Gotts (1977) have described the importance of teaching skills that are functionally related to one another to facilitate generalization. As opposed to teaching separate tasks for each situational area, a common skill is identified, taught, and generalized across task situations. For example, "taking pants off" is a skill that could be taught and generalized to both undressing and toileting situations. A test could be organized around basic operations (e.g., taking off, putting on, grasping) rather than situations (e.g., dressing, toileting). In selecting future item groupings, perhaps designers of tests for SPH children should consider these functional relationships between skill clusters.

Item Sequence

Sailor and Haring (1977) have described the sequencing of test items as "done largely on the basis of some attention to normal developmental milestones and pure speculation" (p. 7). The "optimal" sequence has yet to be validated by research. For this reason, current item sequences vary between tests used with SPH populations. The order of items is generally determined in one or more of the following ways: (a) average age norms, (b) SPH norms, (c) degree of independence achieved, and (d) task analysis.

Developmentally determined sequences may not be appropriate in testing or teaching SPH children. For example, a severely cerebral-palsied child will not be able to learn all of the "normal" skills for walking, but may be able to learn how to move with adaptive equipment. Consequently some severely handicapped children never achieve all of the developmental milestones in an area in which they have a severe disability.

Even if an SPH child were physically able to perform certain developmental pinpoints, two other questions would need to be addressed. Is the pinpoint functionally relevant? Are developmental pinpoints able to discern changes or differences in performance? For example, a normal child between 13 and 15 months of age should be able to build a tower with two cubes (Bayley, 1968; Gesell, 1940; Sheridan, 1968; Slosson, 1964). However, owing to the lack of this task's relationship to independent living, it may not be a relevant one to teach or test. In addition, developmental pinpoints may discern changes for normal children but not for

SPH children. An SPH child may achieve only a few items in a given year. Enough items have to be present so that growth can be measured and greater reliability obtained.

SEQUENCING ACCORDING TO DIFFICULTY

In addressing these problem areas, some test designers have arranged items in increasing order of difficulty for a specific SPH population (e.g., Camelot Behavioral Checklist, Foster, 1974). Difficulty is determined by the percentage of the SPH sample needing training on a particular item. The problem with this approach relates again to the heterogeneity of the SPH population. Given the low incidence and multiplicity of handicaps, homogeneous comparison groups are difficult to obtain.

SEQUENCING ACCORDING TO INDEPENDENCE

Some tests have sequenced items according to the degree of independence achieved or the number of prompts needed for successful performance. This criterion for sequencing is often used in the self-help area. While this approach does relate to independent functioning, it may not consider variation in physical ability. These differences are sometimes mentioned in the test manual. In these cases the teacher or tester must adapt or omit the sequence on the basis of individual differences.

SEQUENCING ACCORDING TO TASK ANALYSIS

Most educators of SPH children are now examining sequences based on their functional impact. "Everyday" tasks are analyzed from two standpoints: the prerequisite skills needed to perform the task and alternative ways of completing the same task. Task analysis is used to determine specific concepts and operations needed to perform a behavior. Using this approach, mastery of each subgoal leads the learner to mastery of the terminal goal. The terminal behavior is described and analyzed backward or forward, with subgoals incorporating each of the basic concepts and operations. Variations based upon physical differences are included in the sequence from an assessment of entry behaviors. Because of the complexity of most basic tasks, lattices have been developed to visually describe the interrelationships among various subcomponents (Smith & Snell, 1978).

Some tests have attempted to sequence items according to this task analytic approach but, because of time constraints, are often unable to provide the number and variation in responses required for a complex terminal behavior due to time constraints. Consequently most assessment devices provide only general guidelines or checklists for the teacher's use in planning more comprehensive programming for individual SPH children.

Test item sequences should meet at least two criteria: (a) the item sequence should relate to a functionally relevant behavior, and (b) the number of items included in the sequence should be sufficient for measuring change. Sailor and Haring (1977) have stated: "Education of the severely/multiply handicapped child is still awaiting the development of well-defined skill sequences across curricula domains. At this point much is up to the teacher's creative use of task analysis" (p. 8).

94 *Assessment Conditions*

Criteria for evaluating assessment conditions usually focus on three questions:

1. Does the condition elicit the "best" response?
2. Is the condition relevant to ultimate functioning?
3. Are condition characteristics systematically varied to ensure generalization?

Haring (1976) has pointed out that the child's best responses are more predictive of future performance. To elicit the "best" response, the Balthazar Scales of Adaptive Behavior (Balthazar, 1971) have listed different procedures for eliciting a specific behavior. If the child does not demonstrate the behavior when an opportunity arises, the observer provides materials or verbal reinforcers upon task completion. If these consequences do not strengthen the desired response, then the observer may provide additional cues or demonstrations before performing the task.

VARIATIONS IN TEST CONDITIONS

Like the Balthazar scale, many tests describe moving from "natural" to more "structured" situations in observing the child's responses. Conditions may be described in terms of location (class or home), persons involved in the assessment (parent, teachers, other professionals), material characteristics (visual, auditory, kinesthetic), the degree of child involvement (none to high), and consequences used (specific reinforcers). Responses are then varied under different testing conditions to determine the "best" condition for the "best" response. Test materials point out the need to evaluate

"typical" or "spontaneously occurring" behavior (BCP, Office of the Santa Cruz County Superintendent of Schools, 1973; Callier-Azusa Scale, Stillman, 1978).

However, some tests list specific task conditions. For example, in drawing a "straight line between two points" on the Callier-Azusa Scale (Stillman, 1978), the child is given two ¼-inch dots, which "are drawn 4 inches apart" (p. 20). Other items on this scale list a variety of objects to be used (e.g., "places or pastes circle, square, tree, house on outline shape of same size," p. 21). Similarly, the Pennsylvania Training Model (Somerton & Turner, 1975) lists certain conditions in the assessment guide for *gross* screening and only general or no conditions for specific behaviors within the competency checklists.

Given the lack of specifically described conditions and the wide variations in conditions, it is difficult to compare the test performance of different SPH children or even compare performances of a given child on the same test. Such variations in testing conditions, though necessary, inhibit standardization. In contrast, if the testing conditions and "best" responses are recorded during assessment, teachers may receive more information in planning appropriate programs than they would receive from a standard score.

"NATURAL" VERSUS "ARTIFICIAL" SITUATIONS

Besides examining condition characteristics that elicit the best responses, test designers have included more situations that are "natural" as opposed to "artificial." For example, Haring (1976) describes human voices and light as more "natural" than pinpricks or intense stimuli in eliciting infant responses. Because successful performance in an artificial condition does not mean that the learner can demonstrate the same behavior in a more natural situation, test manuals emphasize the importance of evaluating children's behavior over time in naturally occurring situations (e.g., mealtimes, bedtimes, free play, community activities).

Problems arise in the amount of time needed for assessment and the absence of certain "natural" situations. Most professionals now agree that an educational assessment of an SPH child generally requires 2 to 4 weeks of observation (Sailor & Haring, 1977). In addition, "naturally" occurring events at home or in other community settings are not always available to the observer. In these cases information is collected through interviews to determine if the behavior occurs (Balthazar, 1971). The current emphasis on collecting data objectively has influenced other designers to limit the use of their tests to certain settings. For example, Stillman (1978) states that "one must be cautious in interpreting findings when the scale is used outside the classroom" (p. 3). Because instruments do not evaluate learner behaviors in all "natural" situations, the trained observer or special education teacher will need to identify relevant situations in which the behavior should "naturally" occur and collaborate with other care givers in providing a comprehensive assessment.

Relevant conditions are a necessary prerequisite to response generalization.

SPH children are often unable to abstract essential characteristics from an irrelevant task to varied environments. For this reason Brown and colleagues (1976) have described the importance of a "zero-degree inference strategy" in assessing performance. Every time the situation changes the SPH child must be reassessed to determine whether or not the response is generalized to the new situation. To ensure this generalization they have described the need to systematically vary the following condition characteristics: (a) person, (b) natural setting, (c) instructional material, and (d) language cue. When the child is able to respond to three different persons in three natural settings using three different instructional materials and three different language cues, the observer can verify that the behavior has been "learned."

Most SPH assessment instruments describe their behavioral checklists as a guide for more extensive observations. The BCP (Office of the Santa Cruz County Superintendent of Schools, 1973) suggests that observations be made "during recess, naps, toileting, bus loading, and meal times as well as during instructional periods" (p. iii). The professional team must assume primary responsibility for varying essential condition characteristics to validate response generalization.

Mastery Criteria

Mastery criteria depend on certain critical behavioral characteristics. First, the behavior must be observable. It would be difficult to determine whether or not a student has obtained a successful performance level unless the performance itself could be observed. Second, the observed behavior should also be measurable or repeatable (i.e., it has beginning and ending points). This characteristic allows the evaluator a means to determine progress and subsequent mastery. A specific condition is often added to further delineate the behavior. For example, Cartwright and Cartwright (1974, p. 53) have described "sharing" in the following manner:

> If the child is playing with a toy and another child approaches and asks to use the toy, the child gives the toy to the other child without any negative verbal statements.

In both instances the behavior can be observed and measured. This objectivity increases the likelihood of agreement between observers as to whether the behavior was actually performed.

Many SPH assessment instruments use short statements in describing behaviors and are often open to interpretation. For example, the item "plays with other children" does not identify observable behaviors for "play." Consequently "play" might be scored differently by different observers. To avoid this problem, some manuals list behavioral objectives or indicate the need to include more than one observer in scoring each item to increase reliability. For example, the Brigance Diagnostic Inventory of Early Development (Brigance, 1978) includes drawings or pictures for some of the behaviorally stated objectives listed in the manual, particularly in the motor areas.

Third, the observed behavior should be sensitive to changes in performance. As mentioned previously, SPH children progress at a much slower rate than other children. "Washing hands" might take an SPH child many months to master. Therefore components of this terminal behavior need to be specified and measured so that progress can be observed. Comprehensive tests attempt to use a greater number of subcomponents for each terminal behavior. The BCP (1973) has 93 points under the heading of "undressing" and "dressing"; the Pennsylvania Training Model (PTM) (Somerton & Turner, 1975) has 75 points under the same heading. In both cases the article of clothing, the degree of independence required, and a task analysis of the operations are considered in developing items.

If the assessment instrument lists behaviors that are refined, observable, and measurable, then performance criteria may be more easily established. The development of criteria depends on (a) the direction of the desired behavioral change, (b) the stage of learning, and (c) ultimate functioning.

PHYSICAL AND TEMPORAL BEHAVIORAL CHANGE

White and Liberty (1976) have described two basic types of behavioral change: physical and temporal. Physical changes may involve the use of different muscles or muscle sequences (topographical change), the intensity of the behavior (force), or the direction of the behavior (locus). Temporal changes include the amount of time a behavior lasts (duration), the number of times a behavior occurs within a unit of time (frequency or rate), or the amount of time between a behavior and some event (latency). The method for collecting data and the specification of criteria will vary depending upon the type of desired behavior change. For example, topographical, locus, and duration changes would need to be described for establishing "attention" criteria. The student would need to be able to lower or raise his or her head to a certain degree (topographical), look at the task or teacher (locus), and focus for a certain period of time (duration). On the other hand, changes in "sharing" might involve turning toward a peer (topographical and locus), speaking softly (force), and giving a toy to the peer (topographical and locus) within 10 seconds (latency).

LEARNING STAGES

Besides including the type of desired change, criteria also need to reflect the stage of learning. Some researchers indicate that there are at least three different learning stages: acquisition, proficiency, and maintenance (Smith & Lovitt, 1976; White & Liberty, 1976). During the acquisition phase the student demonstrates that he or she can accurately perform the desired behavior. Because the SPH child's performance is often inconsistent, acquisition criteria usually include observations over a period of time or trials before mastery is assumed. In addition, Soltman and Rieke (1977) found that one SPH child's mean number of correct responses increased when consecutive trials were changed to intermittent ones. Consequently the nature of the trials may also need to be described in setting an acquisition criterion.

After the acquisition criterion is reached, the student learns to perform the behavior at a faster rate (i.e., proficiency). In this learning stage the student must be provided opportunities for repeated performance in order to attain the proficiency criterion. As described previously, conditions also need to be varied to determine whether the behavior can be demonstrated across situations. To ensure that no inferences are made about performance, these variations should occur in both the acquisition and proficiency stages. Unfortunately "mastery" is often assumed after the acquisition criterion is met within a single setting. In these cases, the probability of maintenance across time is less likely.

Assume a teacher is teaching "housekeeping" skills. The learner is taught initially how to hold and use a broom. Criteria are set for these "holding" and "sweeping" motions. Once the learner can accurately perform these behaviors, criteria are then established for proficiency. At what rate should the learner be able to "grasp," "hold the broom," and "sweep"? Proficiency is attained not only within the classroom but also within the setting in which the behavior is eventually to be performed and maintained (e.g., home, restaurant, motel).

With this example, "ultimate functioning" must obviously be considered in developing performance criteria. Criteria should be similar to those encountered in adult life. Proficiency standards will vary for individual SPH children depending on what is necessary for "successful" living within their immediate environment.

HIT-AND-MISS CRITERION SETTING

Heterogeneity makes establishment of standard criteria for the SPH population difficult. Most often a criterion is determined by observing persons who are already successfully performing the desired behavior. The severity of the disability often makes normal sample comparisons invalid (i.e., proficiency for a "normal" adult may not be necessary for successful living). In addition, homogeneous SPH samples are difficult to obtain. Criterion setting therefore is more "hit and miss" than scientific and depends on individual characteristics.

MEASURING COMPETENCY

Perhaps these problems and a lack of research have influenced the inadequate criteria specification apparent in current SPH assessment instruments. Some tests are simply behavioral checklists, using a binary scoring system. The observed behavior is scored as either present or absent. In some cases, the observer is asked to "guess" whether the learner could perform the behavior in different situations or to provide a structured learning situation (Foster, 1974). Other tests use a scale or continuum for scoring each item. The rater is asked to determine whether the behavior occurs "frequently," "occasionally," or "usually" (Nihira et al., 1974; Sailor & Mix, 1975). Phrases such as "many problems," "great difficulty," "is difficult to reach," and "actively seeks" necessitate judgment by the rater.

Other instruments have attempted to base their competency criteria on a more precise measure of behavioral frequency.

For example, on the BCP, criterion is reached if the behavior is performed at a "75% incidence level." The same is true of the PTM. "No competency" is represented by "0% correct response," "moderate competency" by "25% correct response," "adequate competency" by "75% correct response," and "complete competency" by "100% correct response." Percentages are also computed on the Balthazar scales based on the number of times the behavior is evidenced in "familiar" situations across 10 observations. In addition, the Balthazar and the PTM attempt to examine learning rate or proficiency. The Balthazar asks the rater to record the number of seconds for various "eating" behaviors. The PTM's assessment guide asks the observer to record "the total number of days the task was presented, the number of trials to successfully reach criterion, the total time spent on the task, and the total number of correct responses" (p. 3). However, observational conditions are often not precisely identified. The PTM does attempt to identify whether trials were presented consecutively or over a period of time while the Balthazar does not. Owing to the SPH child's often inconsistent performance, it would be difficult to determine mastery of different learning stages without collecting rate data (i.e., number of behaviors per unit of time) over time and across situations.

FUTURE DIRECTIONS

Assessment of the SPH population is currently more an art than a science. While most tests have provided teachers with a set of basic behaviors, few have developed standard conditions or mastery criteria. For this reason, evaluating or comparing the "appropriateness" of educational programs is difficult. The major problem in developing standardized instruments relates to the heterogeneity and low incidence of the SPH population. Homogeneous subgroups are not easy to obtain. Consequently the Consortium on Adaptive Performance Evaluation (CAPE) developed an assessment and evaluation system for those functioning below the two-year level based on data collected from multiple sites dealing with SPH populations across the nation (Adaptive Performance Inventory). Using this data base, CAPE generated a list of target skills, classified as critical functions or behaviors. It described sequences and interdependencies between these skills, adapting for individual differences. It specified more thoroughly the stimulus and response characteristics of testing conditions. And it established mastery criteria. In addition, a computerized support system is used in the collection of longitudinal data and in the subsequent analysis and revision of the assessment strategy. The final instrument should address some of the current inadequacies present in the assessment of the SPH population. Several future directions for test development have been raised in this article.

Assessment of the SPH population is currently more an art than a science. . . Few tests have developed standard conditions or mastery criteria.

Item Content

Content should focus on basic behaviors and their functional impact. SPH children may eventually function in different settings ranging from an institution to community-based homes with concomitant differences in daily living activities (e.g., no work to semicompetitive employment). Content should reflect the common adaptive behaviors required across multiple situations. In this way, skills learned or assessed are not situationally bound.

Item Sequence

Sequences should be task analyzed from this multiple-setting standpoint and adapted for individual differences. Enough items should be included to facilitate the measurement of progress. Therefore multiple sequences may exist for the same terminal behavior.

Assessment Conditions

Given the zero-degree inference strategy, behaviors should be assessed across several settings to ensure generalization. Conditions will also need to vary for specific severe disabilities. Test designers will need to examine essential stimulus dimensions in determining a relevant set of situations for assessment.

Mastery Criteria

All test items should present behaviors that are observable and measurable. The type of desired change should be evident, completely described, and varied for spe-

100

cific disabilities. Criteria must be established for each stage of learning. An accurate performance in a single situation will not guarantee proficiency or maintenance. To determine various criteria levels, rate data will need to be collected across various settings.

It may be difficult to develop a single standardized instrument that is both comprehensive and sensitive to the extreme variation within the SPH population. However, the complexity of the task should not preclude efforts in this direction. Not many years ago the SPH population was viewed as uneducable and untestable. Views have changed. SPH children *do* learn. Given current technology, the opportunity for the development of more precise instruments in measuring change and planning appropriate educational programs is available. In the future, refined assessment strategies may enhance the probability of each SPH child's success.

REFERENCES

Balthazar, E. *Balthazar scales of adaptive behavior.* Champaign, Ill.: Research Press, 1971.

Bayley, N. *Bayley infant scales of development.* New York: Psychological Corp., 1968.

Bricker, D., Dubose, R., Alberte, P., Berkler, M., Filler, J., Gast, D., Holder, L., Jens, K., Kauffman, J., Sears, J., & Snell, M. Issues in certification for teachers of the severely handicapped. Unpublished manuscript, 1978.

Bricker, D., & Iacino, R. Early intervention with severely/profoundly handicapped children. In E. Sontag, J. Smith, & N. Certo (Eds.). *Educational programming for the severely and profoundly handicapped.* Reston, Va.: Council for Exceptional Children, 1977, 166-176.

Bricker, W. Service of research. In M. Snell (Ed.), *Systematic instruction of the moderately and severely handicapped.* Columbus, Ohio: Charles E. Merrill, 1978, 3-18.

Brigance, A. *Brigance diagnostic inventory of early development.* Woburn, Mass.: Curriculum Associates, 1978.

Brown, L., Branston, M. B., Nietupski, S., Pumpian, I., Certo, N., & Gruenewald, L. A strategy for developing chronological-age-appropriate and functional curricular content for severely handicapped adolescents and young adults. *Journal of Special Education,* 1979, *13,* 81-90.

Brown, L., Nietupski, J., & Hamre-Nietupski, S. Criterion of ultimate functioning. In M. A. Thomas (Ed.), *Hey don't forget about me!* Reston, Va.: Council for Exceptional Children, 1976, 2-15.

Bureau of Education for the Handicapped, United States Office of Education, Section 121.2, 1974.

Cartwright, C. A., & Cartwright, G. P. *Developing observational skills.* New York: McGraw-Hill, 1974.

Dubose, R. Identification. In M. Snell (Ed.), *Systematic instruction of the moderately and severely handicapped.* Columbus, Ohio: Charles E. Merrill, 1978, 3-18.

Foster, R.W. *Camelot behavioral checklist manual.* Parsons, Kans.: Camelot Behavioral Systems, 1974.

Gesell, A. *The first five years of life: A guide to the study of the preschool child.* New York: Harper, 1940.

Guess, D., Horner, R. D., Utley, B., Holvoet, J., Maxon, D., Tucker, D., & Warren, S. A functional curriculum sequencing model for teaching severely handicapped. *AAESPH Review,* 1978, *2,* 203-215.

Haring, N. Infant identification. In M. A. Thomas (Ed.), *Hey, don't forget about me!* Reston, Va.: Council for Exceptional Children, 1976, 16-35.

Haring, N., & Pious, C. Future directions in work with severely and profoundly handicapped persons: An overview. In N. Haring & L. Brown (Eds.), *Teaching the severely handicapped.* New York: Grune & Stratton, 1976, 3-16.

Kauffman, J. M., & Payne, J. S. (Eds.). *Mental retardation: Introduction and personal perspectives.* Columbus, Ohio: Charles E. Merrill, 1975.

McKenzie, H., Hill, M., Sousie, S., York, R., & Baker, K. Special education training to facilitate rural, community-based programs for the severely handicapped. In E. Sontag, J. Smith, & N. Certo (Eds.),

Educational programming for the severely and profoundly handicapped. Reston, Va.: Council for Exceptional Children, 1977, 96-110.

Mercer, J. R. Psychological assessment and the rights of children. In N. Hobbs (Ed.), *Issues in the classification of children* (Vol. 1). San Francisco: Jossey-Bass, 1975.

Nihira, K. Factorial descriptions of the AAMD adaptive behavior scale. In W. A. Coulter & H. W. Morrow (Eds.), *Adaptive behavior: Concepts and measurements.* New York: Grune & Stratton, 1978, 45-57.

Nihira, K., Foster, R., Shellhaas, M., & Leland, H. *American association on mental deficiency adaptive behavior scale.* Washington, D.C.: American Association on Mental Deficiency, 1974.

Office of the Santa Cruz County Superintendent of Schools. *Behavior Characteristics Progression.* Palo Alto, Calif.: VORT Corp., 1973.

Public Law 94-142. *The education for all handicapped children act of 1975.* Washington, D.C.: The National Association of State Directors of Special Education, Inc., 1976.

Sailor, W., & Haring, N. Some current directions in education of the severely/multiply handicapped. *AAESPH Review,* 1977, 2, 3-24.

Sailor, W., & Mix, B. *TARC: Assessment inventory for severely handicapped children.* Lawrence, Kans.: H & H Enterprises, 1975.

Sheridan, M. *The developmental progress of infants and young children.* London: Her Majesty's Stationery Office, 1968.

Slosson, R. *Slosson intelligence test.* New York: Slosson Education, 1964.

Smith, D. D., & Lovitt, T.C. The differential effect of reinforcement contingencies on arithmetic performance. *Journal of Learning Disabilities,* 1976, 1, 32-40.

Smith, P., & Snell, M. In M. Snell (Ed.), *Systematic instruction of the moderately and severely handicapped.* Columbus, Ohio: Charles E. Merrill, 1978, 20-73.

Soltman, S., & Rieke, J. A. Communication management for the non-responsive child: A team approach. In E. Sontag, J. Smith, & N. Certo (Eds.), *Educational programming for the severely and profoundly handicapped.* Reston, Va.: Council for Exceptional Children, 1977, 348-359.

Somerton, M. E., & Turner, K. *Pennsylvania training model individual assessment guide.* Pennsylvania Department of Special Education, 1975.

Stillman, R. *The Callier-Azusa Scale.* Dallas, Tex.: Callier Center for Communication Disorders, University of Texas at Dallas, 1978.

White, O. R., & Liberty, K. A. Behavioral assessment and precise educational measurement. In N. G. Haring & R. L. Schiefelbusch (Eds.), *Teaching special children.* New York: McGraw-Hill, 1976.

Williams, W., & Gotts, E. A. Selected considerations on developing curriculum for severely handicapped students. In E. Sontag, J. Smith, & N. Certo (Eds.), *Educational programming for the severely and profoundly handicapped.* Reston, Va.: Council for Exceptional Children, 1977, 221-236.

Book and Test Reviews

Sara G. Tarver
Curtis C. Dudley-Marling
University of Wisconsin
Madison, Wisconsin

J. Michael Coleman
University of Texas at Dallas
Richardson, Texas

The Dynamic Assessment of Retarded Performers by Reuven Feuerstein. Baltimore: University Park Press, 1979. *413 pages. $24.50.*

One distinction between regular and special educators is the increased emphasis on assessment that is central to the training of teachers of handicapped children. Assessment is an integral component of special education; it is used in planning remedial activities for children and is generic to the identification process. Special educators commonly accept the premise that assessment is a prerequisite for effective instruction. In fact, the need for more efficient assessment is a theme common to many of the articles that appear in this issue of EEQ. Our total acceptance of the importance of assessment to special education overshadows the fact that, periodically, a voice from the wilderness surfaces to question the ultimate benefit of many traditional assess-

0196-6960/80/0013-0103$2.00
© 1980 Aspen Systems Corporation

104

ment activities to the education of handicapped children.

In a companion volume to *Instrumental Enrichment* (see review EEQ 1:2) Feuerstein further details his thoughts on cognitive modifiability while introducing the reader to the assessment device used in conjunction with the Feuerstein Instrumental Enrichment Program. While a majority of the book is devoted to a description of the "Learning Potential Assessment Device," the author allocates considerable space to a critique of standardized, static educational assessment measures and their value to the educational process. He pays particular attention to psychometric assessment and the value of norm-referenced information to the training of handicapped children.

Feuerstein examines sociological issues in norm-referenced testing. He highlights the role of situational factors in test performance and explores the disturbing question of whether psychometric measurement reflects—or creates—inequality. Feuerstein travels ground familiar to special educators in detailing the debilitating effects of handicap labels that are legitimized by psychometric assessment, but he reminds us that the impact of such labels extends further than the child. He contends that labels also influence the teacher's educational goal setting and that these reduced educational expectations artificially limit the child's achievements.

The basic criticisms Feuerstein makes of psychometric measurement are surprisingly not from a social perspective; rather, they deal with fundamental issues in classical testing theory and their incompatibility with educational pursuits.

Most notable of these issues is our predisposition to judge the suitability of an assessment instrument on the basis of its psychometric properties.

Despite its omnipresence in our culture, psychometrics is a young discipline. We are still less than 100 years from the work of Binet. Through most of its development, psychometrics has clung strongly to the belief that the utility of its instruments could best be judged by their statistical properties, particularly reliability and validity coefficients. This preoccupation with statistical rigor, Feuerstein contends, has limited the usefulness of many instruments traditionally used in educational settings. "Striving for increased reliability and validity [in psychometric instruments] may be like an application of medicine that worsens the illness it was supposed to cure" (p. 3).

The key to psychometric rigor, specifically reliability, is stability. For a measure to be reliable, a child's current performance must be predictive of future performance. To accomplish this goal, psychometricians must assess the most stable characteristics of the individual. Of course, the stability of a characteristic is inversely related to its susceptibility to change. And that is Feuerstein's primary criticism of psychometric practice—that psychometric measures assess those characteristics of children that are relatively immutable. Yet for educational purposes, it seems reasonable to examine characteristics of children that are amenable to change, that will be responsive to intervention. This point has been made cogently by Bereiter (1962), whom Feuerstein cites: "The tests available for use in such [educational] evaluations are designed to be good predictors of future status, and in order to be good predictors they must be insensitive to the very changes the educator is trying to produce and measure" (p. 8).

Feuerstein's second criticism is leveled primarily at measures of cognitive functioning. While we use intelligence tests to estimate learning capacity, the tests themselves do not involve active learning. Rather, they provide a sampling of what the child has previously learned. In limiting our view to the products of learning we deny the child the opportunity to demonstrate capacity to learn. What is inevitably lost is that information most critical to the educator—that is, the specifics of the child's learning style, how the child organizes information, what he or she utilizes as learning strategies, how the child approaches abstract problems, and a host of other learning characteristics best described as "meta-learnings." In addition, Feuerstein is concerned that we may ultimately conclude that what is not measured does not exist.

Feuerstein's concerns regarding traditional psychometric assessment are largely reflected in his Learning Potential Assessment Device (LPAD), essentially a measure of cognitive sophistication. While the particulars of the assessment instrument and its role in the Feuerstein Instrumental Enrichment Program are beyond the scope of this review, Feuerstein's departure from traditional psychometric methods in constructing the LPAD are revealing of his conception of relevant assessment. The author himself highlights four major areas in which his

assessment practices are major deviations from traditional testing procedures.

A primary distinction of the LPAD is its use of teaching tasks as assessment items. Rather than inventorying the capacities of the individual, the LPAD focuses on the child's learning potential through interaction in focused learning experiences. The instrument provides the examiner and child with tasks used in a teaching process that allows the examiner to judge the effect of teaching on the ability of the child to master new information. The assessment does not plumb the child's capacity but rather assists the examiner in evaluating how much teaching (and of what type) will be required for an individual to acquire a specific principle or master a specific skill.

As is evident, the role of the examiner administering the LPAD is in opposition to psychometric convention. Within a test-teach-test model the LPAD examiner "conveys to the examinee the meaning of the [assessment] task, the importance of mastering it, his capacity to do so, and finally, by a process of feedback, an ability to select the appropriate behavior leading to success" (p. 104). While this dynamic interaction between examiner and child increases our potential to understand how an individual profits from new information regarding a specific task, the demands it places on the examiner in this situation are considerable.

Two other areas in which the LPAD differs from more conventional assessment relate to aspects of the construction and interpretation of the test. While most assessment views solely the products of learning, Feuerstein is far more in-

106

terested in the process by which a child arrives at a particular answer. Since our task is to modify rather than describe a child's functioning, questions of process are deemed as relevant as those of product. The construction of the assessment instrument has been undertaken so as to facilitate such a process analysis. In regard to test interpretation, it is Feuerstein's position that we can better understand a child's cognitive potential by viewing the peaks of his or her assessment performance, that is, best rather than typical responses.

In keeping with the topic of this issue of EEQ, this review has focused primarily on assessment issues addressed in *The Dynamic Assessment of Retarded Performers*. This narrow perspective should not blind readers to other aspects of the book's contents. The author also discusses his concept of mediated experiences as distinctive from direct experience. He presents evidence regarding the validity of his assessment and remediation approach, including its relevance for educational policymaking. He also outlines his view of the modifiability of human functioning in learning situations. This second work of Feuerstein is a valued addition to *Instrumental Enrichment*, and the two books together constitute a comprehensive overview of the theories and practices of Reuven Feuerstein and his colleagues.

Many of us steeped in the psychometric tradition will remain dubious of the subjective, intrusive nature of Feuerstein's assessment process, as J. McVicker Hunt notes in the foreword of this book. Still, Feuerstein has cogently refocused our attention on the basic rationale of assessment in education—the generation of information relevant for remediation, not simply description. It is a message that cannot be repeated too often.

REFERENCE

Bereiter, C. Using tests to measure change. *Personnel and Guidance Journal*, 1962, *41*, 6-11.

J. Michael Coleman

Language Assessment and Intervention for the Learning Disabled by E.H. Wiig and E.M. Semel. Columbus, Ohio: Charles E. Merrill Publishing Co., 1980. *451 pages. $16.95.*

In the words of the authors, "this book seeks to put the day-to-day management of the learning disabled child with a language disorder squarely within the domain of the classroom teacher." Wiig and Semel have undoubtedly accomplished this goal. In so doing they have amassed a wealth of information about the normal acquisition of language skills and the language problems of learning disabled children that interfere with their acquisition of those skills. Furthermore they have synthesized this information and related it to assessment and intervention in such a way that it can be applied readily. Amazingly, they have done all of this without oversimplifying the highly complex body of knowledge about linguistics and language development.

This comprehensive book is in five parts. The first provides an overview of the language problems of the learning disabled at the early, middle, and upper elementary grades; adolescence; and young adulthood. These language characteristics are discussed in greater detail in appropriate sections throughout the remainder of the book. This initial overview contains excellent language samples that provide real-life examples of these children's language problems and whet the reader's appetite for the more detailed information to come.

The second, third, and fourth parts of this book cover morphology and syntax, semantics, and memory (retention and retrieval). Each part contains sections on characteristics, assessment, and intervention. The characteristics sections contain detailed, but easily readable discussions of normal language development along with summarizing tables that list the language skills and give the ages at which those skills are normally acquired. Characteristics of learning disabled children that are relevant to the particular language skills under discussion are then reiterated and illustrated with additional language samples.

The assessment sections include descriptions and critiques of major assessment instruments, one of which is the recently published Clinical Evaluation of Language Functions (CELF) developed by Semel and Wiig (1980). While the authors modestly refrain from lauding their own test, their descriptions of it lead this reviewer to predict that it will shortly come into wide use and assume a prominent place in language assessment batteries. The CELF adds to extant language tests in distinctive ways. In particular, two of the subtests of word retrieval—

Producing Names on Confrontation and Producing Word Series—are designed to assess language skills that typically have not been assessed. Recent research regarding the information processing of learning disabled children (e.g., short-term memory studies) suggests that word retrieval problems of the type assessed by the CELF may contribute to deficiencies in cognitive functioning. Wiig and Semel discuss the relationship between language and memory deficits in part four, a section that cognitive researchers will no doubt read with particular interest.

While this book's synthesis of characteristics and assessment information is exemplary in and of itself, its greatest contribution lies in the intervention domain. A void of effective materials and techniques for remediating specific oral language problems has been evident for some time; this book fills that void. General task formats that can be applied to the teaching of a variety of skills are discussed. One format—recognition and judgment of correct grammar—may be employed early in the teaching of any skill and may simply require the child to respond "correct" or "incorrect" to stimulus items presented by the teacher. Other task formats require the child to complete sentences, classify and categorize structures, recognize and identify deep structures, normalize scrambled sentences, paraphrase sentences, transform sentences, resolve complex sentences into component sentences, and synthesize component sentences into complex sentences. Specific techniques for accomplishing each of these tasks are provided along with numerous examples.

108

The final part of the book contains chapters on the language demands of reading and the other content areas of the curriculum such as science and social studies. While this final part complements the rest of the book nicely, it is not the book's forte. Assessment and intervention of oral language problems are the book's strong points; in those areas there are no comparable books appropriate for exceptional children with moderate to mild language problems.

Sara G. Tarver

Test of Language Development (TOLD) by P. L. Newcomer & D. D. Hammill. Austin, Tex.: Pro-Ed, 1977. $43.00.

The Test of Language Development (TOLD) is an individually administered, norm-referenced test assessing receptive and expressive competencies in syntax, semantics, and phonology. It was developed for use with children 4-0 to 8-11 years of age and is basically a screening instrument. The TOLD was not designed to provide direct information for remedial instruction but will help identify language deficits in need of a more thorough evaluation. It can also be useful in logging children's progress in specific programs of language instruction.

The TOLD consists of seven subtests: (1) Picture Vocabulary assesses children's receptive vocabulary; (2) Oral Vocabulary measures children's ability to give oral definitions; (3) Grammatical Understanding measures children's ability to comprehend syntactic forms and grammatical markers; (4) Sentence Imitation requires children to imitate sentences provided by the examiner; (5) Grammatical Completion measures children's ability to understand and use common morphologic forms; (6) Word Discrimination assesses children's ability to differentiate between pairs of words differing in only one phoneme; and (7) Word Articulation measures children's ability to produce selected English sounds.

One of the most attractive features of the TOLD is its ease of administration. It can be administered by school psychologists, speech and language clinicians, and teachers. Test administration typically takes from 35 to 40 minutes. The authors of the TOLD should be congratulated for this excellent performance in identifying the limitations as well as the uses of the TOLD in the test manual. If all test authors were as conscientious in indicating the limitations of their instruments there would be far fewer abuses in the field of testing.

Curtis C. Dudley-Marling

The Test of Written Language (TOWL) by D. D. Hammill & S. C. Larsen. Austin, Tex.: Pro-Ed, 1978. $29.50.

The Test of Written Language (TOWL) enables teachers to consistently judge and quantify a variety of student skills thought to comprise written language. The TOWL can be useful in identifying areas of students' written language in need of further evaluation and in documenting students' progress in special writing programs. The subtests of the TOWL use both contrived and spontaneous writing formats to evaluate children's written language.

The TOWL consists of seven subtests: (1) Vocabulary measures the level of a child's vocabulary produced in spontaneous writing samples; (2) Thematic Maturity evaluates a student's ability to express ideas, opinions, and thoughts; (3) Thought Units assesses a child's ability to generate enough meaningful sentences to express thoughts and feelings adequately; (4) Handwriting measures children's skill in forming letters, words, and numerals in a legible manner; (5) Spelling measures a student's ability to spell phonetically regular and irregular words; (6) Word Usage uses a cloze procedure to measure children's ability to use various morphological and syntactic forms in a written context; and (7) Style measures student's ability to adhere to accepted conventions regarding punctuation and capitalization.

The TOWL is a norm-referenced test that can be administered individually or in groups. It was developed for use with children 8-6 to 14-5 years of age. Administration of the TOWL takes approximately 40 minutes.

The TOWL's main deficiency is its scoring procedure. Scoring is fairly difficult and relies on the subjective judgments of the examiner. However, the test manual supplies numerous sample protocols that provide examiners with enough scoring practice to ensure reliability.

The authors of the TOWL have provided teachers with a rare opportunity to obtain a comprehensive and objective description of students' written language. The authors have also done an excellent job indicating both the uses and limitations of their test.

Curtis C. Dudley-Marling

Notices

CONFERENCE ON PIAGETIAN THEORY AND THE HELPING PROFESSIONS

The University Affiliated Program at Childrens Hospital of Los Angeles and the USC School of Education and the Department of Psychology are co-sponsoring a two-day conference at the University of Southern California on "Piagetian Theory and the Helping Professions" on January 17 and 18, 1981. The four main speakers will be Dr. Charles Brainerd of the University of Western Ontario, Dr. Robbie Case of the Ontario Institute for Studies in Education, Dr. Eleanor Duckworth of the Massachusetts Institute of Technology, and Dr. Rochel Gelman of the University of Pennsylvania.

Recent films and videotapes dealing with the Piagetian concepts will be shown. The afternoon sessions will include 100 papers and Piagetian test demonstrations as well as special workshop sessions. Persons interested in attending the 1981 conference should contact: Anne H. Smith, Piaget Conference Coordinator, University Affiliated Program, Childrens Hospital of Los Angeles, P.O. Box 54700, Los Angeles, CA 90054.

Notices featured in EEQ include information on upcoming events and other areas of interest. Please address all material to be considered for publication in Notices to: Editor, Notices, EEQ, Aspen Systems Corporation, 1600 Research Boulevard, Rockville, MD 20850.